The KING IS Coming

Read About It In Revelation

by
David McCord

You may obtain a 64-page leader's guide to accompany this paperback. Order number 41027 from Standard Publishing or your local supplier.

New Life BOOKS

A Division of Standard Publishing
Cincinnati, Ohio 45231
No. 41026

Unless otherwise noted, all Scripture quotations are taken from the *Revised Standard Version* of the Bible, copyrighted 1952.

© 1984 The STANDARD PUBLISHING CO.,
division of STANDEX INTERNATIONAL Corp.

Library of Congress Cataloging in Publication Data
McCord, David M.
  The king is coming.

  1. Bible. N. T. Revelation—Criticism, interpretation, etc.
  I. Title.
BS2825.2.M39   1984   228'.06   83-23671
ISBN 0-87239-670-3 (pbk.)

Printed in U.S.A.   1984

With a deep sense of indebtedness, love,
and appreciation this book is dedicated
to my wife,

WANDA STOFFERAN McCORD

Table of Contents

Blessed is he who reads aloud the words of the prophecy, and blessed are those who hear, and who keep what is written therein; for the time is near.
Revelation 1:3

Revelation 1
Reading and Study Outline

I. The Purpose and Blessing of Revelation (1:1-3)

II. The Author in Exile and in Tribulation (1:4-11)

III. The Vision of the Son of Man (1:12-20)

Getting Ready for Revelation

John and the Vision of the Son of Man
Revelation 1

The artist has painted a birch tree leaning far out over a deep gorge into which a powerful, thundering waterfall is plummeting. On a branch of the tree a robin is perched, seemingly oblivious to the dangers below. The artist has given his painting the title of *Peace,* and his symbolism is apparent.

The book of Revelation is God's symbolic and artistic revelation of His Son Jesus as the King of kings and the Lord of lords, the ultimate Conqueror of evil and the Rewarder of good.

Verse 1 of chapter 1 prepares us for the symbolic nature of the entire book. God provided John with a variety of visions in order "to show" and by which "he made it known" ("signified" in the *King James Version*). By means of visions, signs, and symbols God reveals in this book what we need to know about His Son and about "what must soon take place."

Revelation and *Apocalypse* are synonymous terms, both meaning unveiling or revealing. This is not John's revelation. It is God's revelation *of* Jesus Christ *to* John. God's purpose is to make known His truth, not to hide it; to reveal, not to conceal; to clarify, not to confuse; to unveil, not to veil.

The best principle for interpreting the book of Revelation, therefore, is to look for obvious meanings in light of the simple gospel of Jesus Christ. Speculation on supposed deeper, complex, hidden mysteries of the book is undependable. Neither is a forced literalism appropriate. Revelation is artwork, clearly symbolizing and signifying the things of God. Jesus is neither a lion nor a lamb, although both symbols reveal important truths about Him. Numbers are used symbolically: 7, 24, 666, 1000, 144,000. We must be careful not to become so engrossed in numbers, symbols, and signs that we miss the message they convey.

The Purpose and Blessing of Revelation (1:1-3)

The focus of the book of Revelation is on the person of Jesus Christ and on "what must soon take place." Knowing Jesus as Lord and Savior prepares a person for living today, tomorrow, and forever. Revelation is especially a handbook for living in "the last days." When can we start using this handbook? When will the last days occur? Right now! John did not envision this to be some far-off time, but plainly states that "the time is near."

In one of his letters John explained, "Children, it is the last hour; and as you have heard that antichrist is coming, so now many antichrists have come; therefore we know that it is the last hour" (1 John 2:18). John perceived himself to be living not only in the last days but in the very last hour! The last days began when Christ finished His ministry here on earth, and will continue until He comes again. The Christian era is the last period of time God has given to man, and we are living in it. The book of Revelation is as timely for us today as it was for the Christians of John's day. The big difference is, of course, that time is much closer now to running out entirely. We do not know when Christ will come, but His coming is closer than it ever has been before.

In 1947 the Doomsday Clock first appeared on the cover of the Bulletin of Atomic Scientists. It is set by atomic scientists to symbolize the threat of nuclear holocaust. Originally it was set at seven minutes before midnight. In 1953 it was moved alarmingly close to midnight, due to the development of the H-bomb by both superpowers. It was then relaxed to twelve minutes before midnight in 1972 with the singing of SALT 1. In 1981 it was returned to four minutes before midnight because of worsening relations between the United States and the Soviet Union. That made it 11:56 P.M.! Scientists now have learned one of God's revealed truths: time is running out. "The time is near." God wants us to know we are living in the last days, and He has provided us with a most suitable handbook for that purpose.

8

Not only does God want to prepare us for living in these last days; He also wants to bless us in the process (verse 3). We will be blessed for reading the book of Revelation. You may want to try reading it aloud with a class or group, with your family or a friend. Not only the reader, but also the hearers will be blessed for listening to what is read. But more than that, we will be blessed if we "keep what is written therein."

The purpose of the book of Revelation (and therefore the purpose of this book you are now reading about Revelation), is not just to provide us with knowledge. Rather, it is to motivate us to action, to lead us to do what it says, to make us put it into practice. Certainly Revelation is meant to be informative, but it is also meant to be practical: that is, to affect and to change our way of living in these last days. Otherwise, what is knowledge for?

One day while Dagwood was watching television, his daughter, Cookie, confronted him with a mind-boggling question. "Daddy," she said, "I'm confused. If high school prepares you for college, and college prepares you for life, what does life prepare you for?" A good question, to which Dagwood gave his comically tragic reply, "I'm not prepared to answer that." How sad! And yet he is only reflecting the society in which he lives.

Knowledge is not an end in itself; it prepares you for life. Life is not an end in itself either; it prepares you for eternity. Revelation will help you reach a blessed eternity, not just by hearing what it has to say, but by doing what it has to say. Otherwise, like Dagwood and many others, you will remain deceived and confounded. "But be doers of the word, and not hearers only, deceiving yourselves" (James 1:22).

The Author in Exile and in Tribulation (1:4-11)

The book of Revelation is not meant to promote fear, anxiety, and turmoil, as some seem to take it. Rather, it begins with an offer of grace and peace from God ("who is and who was and who is to come"), from the Holy Spirit ("the seven spirits who are before his throne"), and from Jesus Christ. Notice the three titles given to Christ in verse 5. They identify Him as prophet, priest, and king. He is the "faithful witness" who consistently proclaims God: He is prophet. He is "the firstborn of the dead," who died, was resurrected, ascended on high, and is now our mediator: He is priest. And He is "the ruler of kings on earth": He is king. Through these various roles Christ has loved us, saved us, and given us a new identity as a kingdom of priests (verses 5, 6). Our new purpose is to live for the praise of His glory (verse 6 and Ephesians 1:11, 12).

Jesus is revealed in the beginning of Revelation as He is at the end: "He is coming with the clouds" (verse 7; compare Acts 1:9-11). When He comes again it will not be a visit known only to a few. Rather, "every eye will see him," including "every one who pierced him." That is, non-Christians will see His return as well as Christians, much to the regret of the former. The significance of God's identity as the Alpha and Omega, the Eternal ("who is and who was and who is to come"), and the Almighty, will be seen when we come to the identity of the Son of Man in verses 17 and 18.

Just as John realized that he was living in the "last hour" and that time was ticking quickly away, he also perceived that "the tribulation" was not a phenomenon of the distant future. The tribulation had already begun, and he was personally experiencing it (verse 9). He had been exiled to the Isle of Patmos (see map), perhaps by Emperor Domitian, and probably for refusing to pronounce the required *Kurios Kaisar,* Lord Caesar, or, Caesar is Lord.

An old man now, conceivably in his nineties, John was torn by his exile from family and friends, and from the fellowship of the Christians he loved so much. (According to ancient tradition, this is the same John who was one of the twelve apostles and who wrote the Gospel of John and 1, 2, and 3 John.) Some have thought that as part of his banishment he had to work at hard labor on the island. In any case, it must have been a most discouraging and potentially depressing tribulation that he was suffering. But God was there. And the revelation that God gave John was designed to uplift and to encourage, not only him but us as well, and every Christian in every age who has ever faced the tribulation of this world. It was an encouragement that came from the same Lord who had once told John and others, "In the world you have tribulation; but be of good cheer, I have overcome the world" (John 16:33).

It was on "the Lord's day," which we know as the first day of the week, or Sunday, that John's spiritual encounter with the risen Lord began (verse 10). He was instructed to record what would be revealed to him and to share it with the seven churches listed here and addressed individually in chapters 2 and 3. (See map.) These seven churches seem to be representative of all Christian churches, both then and now, rather than a select group intended to be the exclusive recipients of the revelation. They are every church; they are us.

The book of Revelation is good news for the church, because we

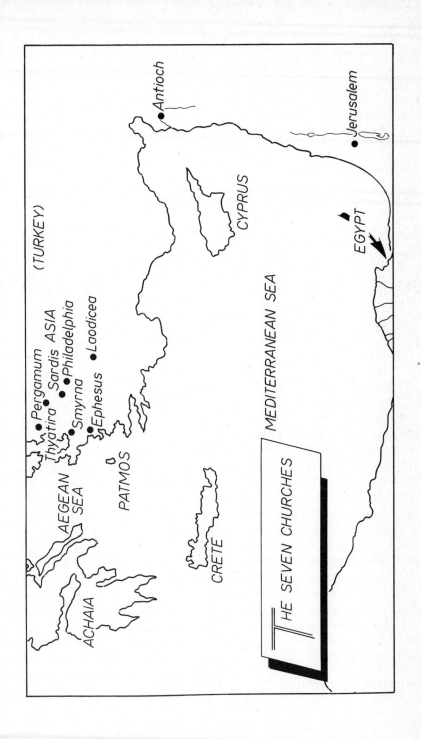

know who Jesus is: prophet, priest, and king. And we know who we are in relation to Him: loved, accepted, forgiven—a kingdom of His priests. But to those outside the church the book of Revelation is bad news, for they have "pierced him" and "will wail on account of him." To John the matter is very clear-cut. "Even so," he declares. "Amen." That's the way it is. Period.

The Vision of the Son of Man (1:12-20)

What John sees first is a vision both spectacular and stunning. It is a vision that stands in stark contrast to the modest and meek Savior who did not cling to equality with God, but emptied himself, took the form of a servant, and was humbly obedient to death on a cross (Philippians 2:5-8). Now He is revealed as the one God has exalted: a mighty king, wise to judge and strong to conquer, the very embodiment of the authority and glory of God. (See chart.)

John is overwhelmed by this vision (verse 17), but Jesus is there to touch and to restore him. An amazing thing now transpires. Jesus reassures John by identifying himself with virtually the same language by which the Lord God has identified himself (verse 8). "Fear not," Jesus says, "I am the first and the last" (Alpha and Omega), "and the living one; I died, and behold I am alive for evermore" (who is and who was and who is to come), "and I have the keys of Death and Hades" (Almighty). It is quite clear what Jesus is saying: *He is God.* This is the way He presents himself to John, to the seven churches, and to you personally.

Some commentators have seen in verse 19 an outline for the entire book of Revelation, although it seems unlikely that it was intended as such. "What you see" would refer to the vision at hand, chapter 1. "What is" would refer to the historical situation at that time; that is, the seven churches, chapters 2 and 3. "What is to take place hereafter" would then refer to all future visions and events, chapter 4-22.

Now that you have seen the vision of the Christ of the Apocalypse through the eyes of John, how will you respond? You may be a little overwhelmed, as John was at first. If so, the Lord is right there to reassure: "Fear not." Of course it is not His intention to scare you, but to inform and prepare you to know Him as God, to obey Him as Lord, to endure tribulation, and to live forever!

The Vision
of
The Son of Man
Revelation 1:12-16

1. Seven golden lampstands (verse 12)
   seven churches (verse 20)

2. One like a Son of man (verse 13)
   Jesus Christ (Daniel 7:13, 14)

3. Long robe with a golden girdle (verse 13)
   royalty

4. Hair white as white wool (verse 14)
   wisdom

5. Eyes like a flame of fire (verse 14)
   piercing judgment

6. Feet like burnished bronze (verse 15)
   purity and power

7. Voice like the sound of many waters (verse 15)
   authority

8. Seven stars (verse 16)
   angels of churches (verse 20)

9. A sharp two-edged sword (verse 16)
   the word of God

10. Face like the sun in full strength (verse 16)
    deity, glory of God

He who has an ear,
let him hear what the Spirit says
to the churches.
Revelation 2:7

Revelation 2, 3
Reading and Study Outline

  I. Ephesus: Right but Cold (2:1-7)
 II. Smyrna: Poor but Rich (2:8-11)
III. Pergamum: Faithful but Tolerant (2:12-17)
IV. Thyatira: Improved but Compromising (2:18-29)
 V. Sardis: Reputable but Dead (3:1-6)
VI. Philadelphia: Weak but Strong (3:7-13)
VII. Laodicea: Lukewarm but Hopeful (3:14-22)

God Knows Your Church

The Seven Churches of Asia
Revelation 2, 3

God's dwelling place, the church, may not be what it is meant to be or what it is often thought to be, for it is "a spiritual house" (1 Peter 2:5), not a structure made with hands. A youngster was visiting relatives in New York City and they took him to see the great cathedral where they worshiped. Looking around in wide-eyed wonder he whispered, "God sure has a nice house to live in, doesn't He?"

The building may obscure our vision of the church in which God really lives, but God's vision is not obscured. He perceives the church exactly as it is, for He sees with eyes "like a flame of fire." As the Son of Man addresses each of the seven churches mentioned in chapters 2 and 3 of Revelation He comments, "I know your works," or "I know your tribulation," or "I know where you dwell." God knows His church, which means that God knows *your* church, which means that God knows *you.*

The letters to the seven churches should be taken as personal messages to the church today—to each of us who belong to the church. Of course these letters are directed to specific, historical churches in specific, historical cities. (See the map in chapter 1.) John probably knew each of these congregations personally and even may have spent some time ministering to each one. At the same time, the seven should be seen as representative churches.

What God said to them He has said to His church throughout history, and He is saying to His church today. It is a message to you and me.

Basically the message is this: God knows His church and is deeply concerned for its (our) spiritual well-being. He sees what is good and what is bad, urging us to faithfulness on the one hand and demanding repentance on the other.

With few exceptions, each of the seven letters to the seven churches is divided into seven parts:

1. The address: the name of the city to which it is sent.
2. The sender: a description of Christ.
3. The good qualities of the church.
4. The bad qualities of the church.
5. The need of the church: an exhortation.
6. The hope or promise to "him who conquers."
7. The plea to the church: "Hear what the Spirit says."

These messages are indicated very briefly in the chart on the next page. It plainly shows four exceptions to the above classification. There is nothing bad to be said about the churches of Smyrna and Philadelphia, and there is nothing good to be said about the churches of Sardis and Laodicea.

Ephesus: Right but Cold (2:1-7)

Ephesus was a major crossroads, the capitol of Asia, and the location of the famous temple of Diana, one of the seven wonders of the ancient world. This city was a center of idolatry and wickedness, yet the Christians there had worked hard and remained faithful to all that was true and right. They would not tolerate wicked men or false doctrine.

Unfortunately, in their strong stance for the truth, they had "abandoned the love you had at first" (verse 4). They had acted out of duty, not compassion. Like many Christians since then, they seemed to love the truth more than they loved people. They had become cold and calloused.

Lack of love is a serious crime. Loveless Christians are told to repent, or, says Jesus, "I will come to you and remove your lampstand from its place" (verse 5). Just how serious could that be? The very purpose of the church is to be a lampstand (Revelation 1:20), holding up the light by which men can find their way to God. To

The Seven Churches

	Ephesus 2:1-7	Smyrna 2:8-11	Pergamum 2:12-17	Thyatira 2:18-29	Sardis 3:1-6	Philadelphia 3:7-13	Laodicea 3:14-22
TO							
FROM	The Son of Man 2:1	The risen Lord 2:8	The righteous judge 2:12	The conquering Lord 2:18	The Lord of the church 3:1	The holy and true one 3:7	The true Witness 3:14
GOOD	Resists 2:2, 3, 6	Suffers 2:9, 10	Affirms 2:13	Serves 2:19		Endures 3:8	
BAD	Cold 2:4		Tolerant 2:14, 15	Tolerant 2:20-23	Dead 3:1		Lukewarm 3:15-17
NEED	Repent 2:5	Be Faithful 2:10	Repent 2:16	Hold Fast 2:24, 25	Repent 3:2, 3	Hold Fast 3:11	Repent 3:19
HOPE	Life 2:7	No second death 2:11	New name 2:17	Rule 2:26-28	White garments 3:4, 5	Pillar 3:12	Fellowship 3:21
PLEA	Hear 2:7	Hear 2:11	Hear 2:17	Hear 2:29	Hear 3:6	Hear 3:13	Hear 3:22

lose their lampstand would be to lose their very purpose for existence, to cease being the church. Right doctrine alone is no sufficient lighthouse for lost souls. Love also is needed.

Zig Ziglar in his motivation speeches has popularized the saying, "People don't care what you know until they know that you care." Right doctrine is good and necessary and must not be compromised; but love also is of the essence, and the lack of love calls for repentance.

Smyrna: Poor but Rich (2:8-11)

Smyrna was a seaport city about thirty-five or forty miles north of Ephesus. There a temple had been built to honor Emperor Tiberius. The Christians of Smyrna were bitterly opposed both by Jews and by heathen, but the risen Lord assured them He knew of their tribulation and poverty ("but you are rich") and how they were being slandered. The "synagogue of Satan" mentioned in verse 9 (and in 3:9) evidently was a congregation of Jews who claimed to worship and obey God, but who, by opposing the church, were serving Satan's purposes, not God's.

The wickedness of these Jews is exemplified in a story that has come down to us from the second century. Polycarp was a disciple of John who became bishop of the church at Smyrna. He was burned at the stake by Roman authorities. The Jews of Smyrna were so zealous for his execution that they helped gather firewood with which to burn him *on the Sabbath!*

Perhaps this was part of the suffering and tribulation the Lord warned the Christians of Smyrna about. It would last for "ten days," which probably means a relatively short period of time rather than literally that number of days. Some of the Christians would be imprisoned, and some would die. Theirs was a good church, not receiving any criticism. Yet the Lord did not offer to prevent the tribulation that was to come. Rather, He told them not to be afraid of martyrdom, for they would receive the crown of life and not be hurt by the second death. The second death is the eternal punishment that awaits those who reject Jesus (Revelation 20:14, 15).

The same message that encouraged them is meant also to encourage us. Physical suffering, economic setback, or religious opposition may seem unbearable. But really it is nothing compared to the second death, and you are safe from that! In other words, don't fear persecution. Fear God. It is best to be faithful to Him even if it costs you your life.

Pergamum: Faithful but Tolerant (2:12-17)

Continuing north from Smyrna we come to Pergamum, where there was a temple built to the honor of Caesar Augustus, the reigning Caesar when Christ was born. The Lord knew it was not easy to be a Christian in Pergamum, for it was a center of Satanism, idolatry, and emperor worship—a "throne" seat, as a county seat is a center of government. Nevertheless, the Christians in Pergamum had affirmed their faith, even in the face of death.

The problem with the Pergamum Christians was that they were willing to tolerate false teaching and sinful living. Numbers 25:1-3 tells how some Israelites were led into idolatry and immorality. Numbers 31:15, 16 indicates that Balaam suggested this. Some people at Pergamum were following the same course. The Nicolaitans wanted to compromise with heathenism, and some students think there was another sect of Balaamites at Pergamum. At Ephesus the Christians hated the works of the Nicolaitans (Revelation 2:6), but at Pergamum the Christians seemed to be saying, "What they do is their own business." Jesus told them to repent of such apathy. If they would not, He said, "I will come to you soon and war against them." With His word, the sword of His mouth, Jesus would defeat those of sinful lives. The implication seems to be that tolerance and apathy are unacceptable; confrontation and conversion are expected. The Nicolaitans must be converted or they will be destroyed. Part of the responsibility of the church is to reclaim those who go astray.

The conquerors at Pergamum were promised three things:

1. "Hidden manna": Christ, the bread of life, would be with them forever.

2. "A white stone": this was a sign of forgiveness and acquittal. A black stone would indicate guilt.

3. "A new name," a new identity: "It does not yet appear what we shall be" (1 John 3:2).

With the Pergamum Christians we have been warned. Do we wink at sin and excuse sinners, saying, "That's their business"? That attitude calls for repentance. Confronting sin and converting sinners is our business.

Thyatira: Improved but Compromising (2:18-29)

Southeast from Pergamum lay the relatively small city of Thyatira. As far as we know there was no emperor cult there, but the ancient pagan religions of Asia held sway. The church there had made considerable improvement: "your latter works exceed the first" (verse

19). This was in five areas: works, love, faith, service, and endurance. Quite a commendation!

Like Pergamum, however, Thyatira was tolerant of evil. The "Jezebel" mentioned here may have been an individual by that name or one so called because she was like the Jezebel who was notorious in Israel's history (1 Kings 16:30, 31). Or possibly the name refers to a cult that was seducing Christians into false belief and immoral conduct. Jezebel and her associates must repent. If they would not, judgment would be executed, judgment severe but just and deserved. But to those holding fast to Christian faith and godly living there was the promise of power, of ruling, and of "the morning star," Christ himself (see Revelation 22:16).

It is good to see a church or an individual Christian improving, sharpening skills, expanding ministry, growing. But if there is a lack of discipline in a Christian's life or in the corporate life of a congregation, especially in the areas of false doctrine and immorality, look out! Such unfaithfulness constitutes spiritual adultery, and God will punish it severely. Faithfulness must accompany progress.

Sardis: Reputable but Dead (3:1-6)

The notable feature of Sardis was the fortress located on a high hill within its city walls. It looked formidable and apparently impregnable. Yet on two different occasions Sardis had been invaded and conquered: by Cyrus about 549 B.C. and by Antiochus the Great about 218 B.C. How was it possible? In both cases it was due to a lack of vigilance on the part of the watchmen. The key word for Sardis, therefore, was "Awake!" "If you will not awake, I will come like a thief, and you will not know at what hour I will come upon you" (verse 3).

There is hope even for a "dead" church! Sardis had a good reputation. The congregation was known as being "alive," but nothing could have been further from the truth. But there is a cure for spiritual death, and that is repentance. Christ could see in this church something worth building on, a remnant that could be strengthened, a "few names" of "people who have not soiled their garments" (verse 4). With Christ as Lord of the church there is always hope, and judgment can be reversed at any time before Jesus comes again: "I will not blot his name out of the book of life" (verse 5). (Compare Jonah 3:10.)

The message is clear: do not count on religious appearances, affiliations, or showy activities for God's approval. It is hypocritical.

Christ saw right through the facade of the Pharisees—beautiful in outward appearance but full of dead men's bones within (Matthew 23:27). Sardis shared the same guilt. The temptation to hypocrisy is a constant problem for the church. Repentance and honest confession to God are the cure.

Philadelphia: Weak but Strong (3:7-13)

This city was noted for its strategic location. It was the "gateway" to the plateau region of Phrygia, central Asia, and the cities of that area. The builders of modern railroads used this same area as their point of departure to ascend to the plateau. Perhaps it is this factor that is hinted at by the "open door" of verse 8.

Philadelphia was not a strong church, but it used its opportunities and was faithful to its purpose. Even the "synagogue of Satan" came to respect this little congregation. The Christians of Philadelphia were to be spared persecution, and each conqueror was to be made "a pillar in the temple of my God" (verse 12). Some pagan temples housed pillars or pedestals bearing the names of noteworthy warriors or citizens and sometimes sculptured busts. The faithful Christian is to be made a permanent fixture in the temple of God, bearing God's name to honor Him.

Philadelphia's strength lay not in her size, but in her opportunities for witness and mission. In a sense, every Christian and every church is strategically located to serve as a "gateway" through which someone may be led to Christ. Think about it. Your strength for success comes neither from size nor from self, but simply from using the opportunities God gives you to be His faithful witness.

Laodicea: Lukewarm but Hopeful (3:14-22)

Laodicea was a major banking center whose main products were woolen cloth and an eyesalve with apparent medicinal properties. Commerce enhanced the city's wealth. When Laodicea was devastated by an earthquake in A.D. 61, the emperor obligingly offered financial assistance. But the people of Laodicea refused to accept. They thought they did not need the emperor, or God, or anybody. They were wealthy in material things, but they were spiritually impoverished. Evidently the church shared the character of the city.

This church was "neither cold nor hot," but a nauseous "lukewarm" (verses 15, 16). Apathy and mediocrity are sickening to the Lord and cannot be retained within His body. But there is an alternative to being outcasts. There is hope even for a lukewarm church like the one in Laodicea. It is to exchange our perishable wealth for His imperishable (verse 18). It is to repent and accept His loving discipline for our lives (verse 19). And it is to respond to His beautiful invitation to enter into a personal and intimate relationship with Him, like friends sitting down to a meal together (verse 20). God wants us to "get on fire" for Him. Mediocrity is unacceptable.

"He who has an ear . . ." Are you hearing what God is saying to His church? Do some serious evaluating of your church and of your life. What do you find there that is good and pleasing to the Lord? Hold fast to it and don't let loose! What do you find there that is bad and needs changing? By all means repent and actively pursue God's will and His discipline.

The rewards for the faithful and disciplined Christian life are incredible! "He who conquers, I will grant him to sit with me on my throne, as I myself conquered and sat down with my Father on his throne" (3:21).

"He who has an ear, let him hear what the Spirit says to the churches."

*Holy, holy, holy, is the Lord God Almighty,
who was and is and is to come!*
Revelation 4:8

Relevation 4, 5
Reading and Study Outline

I. The One, the Four, and the Twenty-Four (4:1-11)
   The First Song (4:8)
   The Second Song (4:10, 11)

II. The Worthiness of the Lamb (5:1-14)
   The Third Song (5:8-10)
   The Fourth Song (5:11, 12)
   The Fifth Song or Saying (5:13)

A Time to Sing

The Throne and the Lamb
Revelation 4, 5

Chapters 4 and 5 of Revelation are rather like a musical extrava-ganza. They feature "The Four Living Creatures" along with the "The Twenty-Four Elders." Their musical back-up is provided by "Myriads of Angels" whose singing, I might add, is absolutely out of this world! The main attraction, however, is "The Slain Lamb" about whom, along with His Father, five songs are sung.

Why all the singing, particularly at this point in Revelation? Shouldn't that come at the end, when the battle is done and the victory is won?

When our daughter, Cindy, was three years old we visited the church at Heaton, North Carolina, where I had previously served as the minister. She had not sat with both her parents in church before, nor had she observed a communion service, since she was always in the nursery in the church we then served.

Cindy watched very intently as the emblems were passed and as I ate the bread and drank from the cup. Then I bowed my head to meditate. In a moment there was a tug on my coat sleeve. I tried to ignore it, but I could sense two little eyes staring at me. The tug came again. This time I leaned low to hear her whisper. "Daddy," she asked, "what did that do to you?"

Worship does do something to us, or for us. Not only is worship at the end of the week a culmination of our walk with the Lord, an outburst of thanksgiving, joy, and praise; it is also a preparation for the week to come, providing us with inspiration, encouragement, and direction, enabling us to continue our walk with the Lord in the new week.

The songs and worship of Revelation 4 and 5 are preparing John (and us) for what is to come. Soon he will witness the fearful judgment of God: the seven seals, trumpets and plagues, the two beasts, the harlot, Armageddon, and all the rest. Revelation can be very frightening and depressing unless it is kept in proper perspective. Through worship John is prepared, and we are prepared, for whatever lies ahead. So now is the time to sing and to worship and to acknowledge that God is God and that Christ is the Lamb that was slain. Because God is God, we are sure His cause will be victorious. Because Jesus gave His life, we are sure we are redeemed from sin and death to share His victory.

The One, the Four, and the Twenty-Four (4:1-11)

First, John saw the one upon the throne. What he saw was not distinct features of a person, but an array of jewel-like colors: jasper (an opaque quartz that is found in various shades of purple, blue, and green), carnelian (a red quartz), and an emerald green rainbow. It must have been spectacular in beauty.

Around the throne were the twenty-four elders wearing white garments, crowned with gold, and sitting on thrones. The number twenty-four suggests the twelve tribes of Israel plus the twelve apostles of Christ. Since white garments are the clothing of the redeemed (Revelation 7:13, 14), the twenty-four elders may be representative of all the redeemed, both of the Old and the New Testaments. The throne is the center of both power and peace (verses 5, 6a).

Next are seen the four living creatures, "full of eyes in front and behind" (all-seeing and all-wise), and "each of them with six wings" (ready for service and quick to respond). Many symbolic meanings have been seen in the four living creatures, four of which I will share with you here. (See the chart on the next page.)

1. The four living creatures may be superior beings intended to represent all living creatures: the lion representing wild beasts; the ox, domestic animals; the "face of a man," mankind; and the eagle, birds of the air.

2. The four may be representative of Christ: the lion representing His authority; the ox, His sacrifice (since it is a sacrificial animal); the man, His humanity; and the eagle, His divinity.

26

CHRIST'S DIVINITY

MARK

CHRIST'S SACRIFICE

DOMESTIC BEASTS

BIRDS

JOHN

GOD'S LOVE

GOD'S SOVEREIGNTY

GOD'S INCARNATION

GOD'S POWER

WILD BEASTS

MATTHEW

CHRIST'S AUTHORITY

LUKE

MANKIND

CHRIST'S HUMANITY

3. Some see in the four living creatures the four Gospels: the lion representing Matthew (authority); the ox, Mark (sacrifice); the man, Luke (humanity); and the eagle, John (divinity).

4. A fourth possibility and the most likely, it seems to me, is that these are representative of the attributes of God: the lion representing His power; the ox, His love; the man, His incarnation; and the eagle, His sovereignty. This is one of the places where the abundance of possibilities warns us not to be too sure. If the meaning were made clear in the Scriptures, careful scholars would not have four different opinions. I have my favorite among the four; but you may choose another, or perhaps one that is not included in the four. But the record plainly tells what the four living creatures were doing. We all agree on that, and in that we find the undoubted message that this particular part of Revelation has for us.

These four creatures (whatever they represent) never cease to bring God praise: "Holy, holy, holy, is the Lord God Almighty, who was and is and is to come!" (verse 8). (Facts about this and the other songs in this section are shown in chart form on the next page. This shows who is singing in each case, how many are singing, to whom they are singing, the subject of their song, and the reason they sing.)

Whenever the four living creatures sing, which is without ceasing, the twenty-four elders respond with a song of their own. Written as follows, this hymn may be sung to the tune of "Jesus, the Very Thought of Thee."

> Worthy art Thou, our Lord and God,
>   To receive praise and pow'r;
> For Thou didst create all that is,
>   And by Thy will, they are.

If this is one of the songs that the redeemed sing in Heaven, maybe it is a good idea to start practicing! Why not see if you can get some of the other songs in these chapters to fit tunes that you already know? They will enrich your worship.

Not only do the twenty-four elders sing, but they also "cast their crowns before the throne" (verse 10). Will we receive crowns when we get to Heaven? Perhaps so, but if we do it will not be for our own glory. The crowns are used here in an act of worship, for the glory of God.

Songs of Revelation 4 and 5

Scripture	Singers	Number	Person	Subject	Reason
4:8	Creatures	4	God	Holiness	Eternal
4:10, 11	Elders	24	God	Worthiness	Creator
5:8-10	Creatures and Elders	28	Christ	Worthiness	Redeemer
5:11, 12	Angels	Myriads of Myriads	Christ	Worthiness	Slain to Redeem
5:13	All Creation	All	Both God and Christ	Praise	Worthy

The Worthiness of the Lamb (5:1-14)

God holds a scroll that has been completed, written on both the front and the back. It is finished and it is sealed. In ancient times the seal served a dual purpose. It identified the author and sender of the document, and it served as a warning against unauthorized opening or use of the document. It was "official." When the scroll is displayed, the question is this: Who is authorized to open and read it? (verse 2).

There is a dramatic and suspenseful moment as the search begins for an authorized one "in heaven or on earth or under the earth" (verse 3). The search appears fruitless, and John weeps. The book or scroll is apparently the book of God's justice, or judgment. If there is no one to open the book there will be no justice. How very sad indeed!

One of the elders then comforts John with the assurance that there is one who is worthy. His credentials are in order. He is the Messiah of the Old Testament ("the Lion of the tribe of Judah, the Root of David") and He is the Savior of the New Testament ("has conquered") (verse 5).

When the Lamb appears it looks as if He has been mortally wounded, but here He is standing and walking. Undoubtedly, this is the Lamb of God who was crucified and raised from the dead. The picture we see of Christ here is a symbol, not a photograph. We must not think of Him as a grotesque-looking seven-horned, seven-eyed lamb. Rather, the horns tell us of His power and the eyes tell us of His wisdom, and that He is filled with the Spirit of God. The fact that He was slain reminds us that He gave His life to redeem us for His kingdom.

When the Lamb receives the scroll the suspense is ended. The four living creatures and the twenty-four elders now form a combined choir, accompanied by the harps of the elders. They sing to praise the worthiness of Christ as Redeemer, "for thou wast slain and by thy blood didst ransom men for God" (verse 9).

(Just as an aside, since there seems to be so much singing and harp-playing in Heaven, I think I will need about the first ten thousand years for music lessons. But I am sure it will be time well spent. On second thought, maybe God will grant us non-musicians instant musical skills. That would be Heaven!)

The music now swells to a crescendo. At first there were only four singers, then twenty-four, then twenty-eight. Now they are joined by "myriads and myriads and thousands of thousands" of angels. Their song seems to be a chorus of the song that has just been sung to praise the worthiness of Christ as Redeemer: "Worthy is the Lamb!" (verse 12).

The crescendo is made complete as every creature in all creation joins in praising both the Father and the Son (verse 13). The four living creatures add an "Amen!" (so be it), affirming that indeed "blessing and honor and glory and might for ever and ever" belong to God and the Lamb. There can be no doubt that the Lamb is worthy to open the seals. "And the elders fell down and worshiped" (verse 14).

"When I get to Heaven gonna play on my harp, gonna sing all over God's Heaven," says an old spiritual. Such is the picture that closes chapter 5. But we also need to worship God right now because He is worthy of our praise and because we need the experience of worship to prepare us for what lies ahead. Now is a time to sing.

*He rode out as a conqueror
bent on conquest.
Revelation 6:2*

Revelation 6:1 – 8:6
Reading and Study Outline

I. The First Six Seals (6:1-17)
    1. The White Horse of Conquest (6:1, 2)
    2. The Red Horse of War (6:3, 4)
    3. The Black Horse of Famine (6:5, 6)
    4. The Pale Horse of Death (6:7, 8)
    5. The Martyrs' Cry for Vengeance (6:9-11)
    6. The Worldwide Calamity (6:12-17)

II. The 144,000 and the Innumerable Multitude (7:1-17)

III. The Seventh Seal (8:1-6)

The Beginning of the End

The Seven Seals and the 144,000
Revelation 6:1–8:6

So far Revelation may seem to be a rather ordinary book of the Bible. In chapter 1 we saw a vision of the Son of Man. The next two chapters were warnings to the seven churches to repent, along with encouragement to hold fast. Chapters 4 and 5 contain the beautiful hymns of the redeemed. You may feel like the man who was falling from a forty-story building. As he passed the twentieth floor he was heard to say, "So far, so good!"

Comfortably we have passed the glorious songs. Now as the Lamb takes the scroll with the seven seals and opens them, we begin to see the justice and wrath of God poured out upon the wickedness and godlessness of men. It is the beginning of the end.

The First Six Seals (6:1-17)
1. The white horse of conquest (verses 1, 2)

The first seal is opened. At the command of one of the four living creatures a rider on a white horse comes forward. This rider is similar to Christ when He comes on a white horse (Revelation 19:11-16). Some students think this rider too is Christ. But some think he is antichrist, whom God used to punish the wicked. If so, the crown he wears is not his to keep. His is a borrowed authority for a brief time. In any case, the rider on a white horse represents a conqueror.

2. The red horse of war (verses 3, 4)

The red horse represents war and bloodshed. If the rider of the white horse is not Christ, his bow may represent very limited warfare or even a "bloodless coup." Now comes a rider armed with a great sword, and the battle intensifies. It is a sword of destruction, and peace is taken away. In its place there are wars, riots, and murders.

3. The black horse of famine (verses 5, 6)

Famine often follows war, and black suggests the pall of death. The third rider carries a balance to be used in measuring out the meager food supplies. Common foods like wheat and barley are hardest hit, while oil and wine are unaffected. The inflation rate becomes unbearable and unaffordable. Typically eight quarts of wheat could be bought for a denarius, a day's wages. Now it is a meager one quart for a day's wages! The same ratio holds true for barley. There is a stark contrast here between former plenty and present want, a famine that leads to increased suffering, starvation, and death.

4. The pale horse of death (verses 7, 8)

Death comes riding on a pale horse, followed closely by Hades, the abode of the dead. At this stage of judgment Death's power is limited to one-fourth of the earth. Added now to war and famine are disease, which typically accompanies famine, and wild beasts. Ferocious animals begin preying on mankind.

As the first four seals are opened, the four horsemen of the apocalypse respond in obedience to the four living creatures who give the command, "Come!" It is important to see that the four riders are under command and not themselves in full control. In fact, it is the Lamb who is opening the seals and thus is truly in control of all that is taking place. It is by His will, or at least His permission, that the horsemen ride.

5. The martyrs' cry for vengeance (verses 9-11)

For the martyrs whose lives have already been sacrificed, there is both good news and bad news. The bad news is that there will yet be more martyrs. The good news is that the injustice they have suffered will finally be avenged. In the meantime their consolation is the white robe of righteousness, and a time of rest. At the final judgment, justice will be made complete and the righteous will be vindicated.

6. The worldwide calamity (verses 12-17)

A worldwide calamity now occurs, beginning with "a great earthquake" (verse 12). "Every one" (verse 15), that is, all who have reason to fear "the wrath of the Lamb" (verse 16), look for a place to hide. It is not the calamity they wish to escape, but His wrath. But there is no place to hide.

Does the sixth seal represent the end of time? Many students think it does. Note how much this catastrophe is like the one described in Matthew 24:29-31, in which Jesus appears in power and sends His angels to gather His people. It is similar also to the end of the world described in 2 Peter 3:10. In the catastrophe introduced by the sixth seal the wicked are convinced that final judgment is upon them. Desperately they try to hide from the wrath of God and the Lamb, "for the great day of their wrath has come."

If this is indeed the end, then we see in the midst of catastrophe 144,000 Jewish servants of the Lord marked with a seal (7:1-8), and then an innumerable multitude of redeemed people gathered to their eternal home with God (7:9-17).

However, there is another seal to be opened. It may be that the catastrophe of the sixth seal is only the beginning of the end. In that case the visions of chapter 7 come as an interlude. They reassure John, and all Christians, that ultimately and eternally they are safe because they have been sealed as God's servants. From this point of view we shall look briefly at the seventh chapter.

The 144,000 and the Innumerable Multitude (7:1-17)

Christians experience the calamities and tragedies of this world just as non-Christians do. John had heard Jesus explain it this way: "In the world you have tribulation; but be of good cheer, I have overcome the world" (John 16:33). Although Christians do not escape tribulation, they are sealed for eternity. So cheer up! That's good news!

The seal is the Holy Spirit, as we see in Ephesians 1:13, 14:

> In him [Christ] you also, who have heard the word of truth, the gospel of your salvation, and have believed in him, were sealed with the promised Holy Spirit, which is the guarantee of our inheritance until we acquire possession of it, to the praise of his glory.

Every Christian is born of the Spirit (John 3:5, 6), gifted with the Spirit (Acts 2:38), indwelt by the Spirit (1 Corinthians 6:19), and is living and walking by the Spirit (Galatians 5:25). The Spirit is the common experience of every Christian's life. He identifies the Christian as surely as if His name were marked upon one's forehead (verse 3). The Holy Spirit is the mark and the seal of the Christian life.

The Seven Seals

Revelation		Who	What	Why	Where
6:1, 2	1	Rider on White Horse	Bow, Crown	Conquest	Earth
6:3, 4	2	Rider on Red Horse	Sword	War	Earth
6:5, 6	3	Rider on Black Horse	Balance	Famine	Earth
6:7, 8	4	Rider on Pale Horse	Sword, Famine, Disease, Beasts	Death	Earth
6:9-11	5	Martyrs	Robes	Wrath	Heaven
6:12-17	6	Everyone	All Creation	Wrath	Earth
7:1-17		Interlude: the 144,000 and the innumerable multitude			
8:1-6	7	Angels	Trumpets	8:6—11:19	Earth

Who are the 144,000? Before you give a literal interpretation to the number, remember the symbolic nature of these visions. Does the earth really have "four corners"? (verse 1). The 144,000 are redeemed Jews, from every tribe of Israel. The 144,000 is not necessarily an exact count. It represents all the Jews who are to be saved, whatever that actual number may finally be. Even the list of tribes given here should be taken symbolically, since Levi is included, though usually left out in listing the tribes; and Dan is omitted, though usually included. The reasons for this are greatly debated but really unknown.

The 144,000, however, are not the only ones who are in Heaven praising God. John sees also "a great multitude . . . from every nation, from all tribes and peoples and tongues" (verse 9). In other words, Gentiles as well as Jews are present in this vision. All have suffered through tribulation (verse 14) and have been faithful unto death. All are wearing the white robes of the redeemed (verses 9, 13), and all are praising God.

Additional assurance and comfort are given to John, and to us, through the beautiful words of verses 15-17. (Compare Revelation 21:1-4.) Because we are marked and sealed for the day of redemption, we are ready to endure whatever trials and tribulations may lie ahead. Now we are ready for the opening of the seventh seal.

The Seventh Seal (8:1-6 or 8:1)

The opening of the seventh seal brings silence. There are two ways of looking at this. Our choice depends on our view of the last part of chapter 6. We may suppose the great events of chapter 6 are those that accompany Christ's coming as described in Matthew 24:29-31. Then in chapter 7 we see Christ's people in their eternal home after His coming. In that case we see the seventh seal ushering in a silence that symbolizes eternal rest. It is like a period. The record of the seven seals is ended. Verse 2 of chapter 8 then begins the record of another series of visions. These foretell in another way what is foretold by the seven seals.

For this study, however, we have chosen another view. We are supposing that chapter 6 records only the beginning of the end, that in the midst of tumult the visions of chapter 7 are given to assure us of future tranquility, and then the tumult continues as recorded in chapter 8. From that point of view we now look at chapter 8.

The seventh seal brings silence. There is no sound at all. There is absolute stillness, breathtaking, suspenseful, frightening! There is a sense of dread in the air in anticipation of what is to follow. Seven angels stand poised like silent sentinels, muscles tense and nerves taut, ready for the signal that will put them on the offense.

Fire from the altar is thrown to the earth. In terrifying contrast to the silence that preceded, "there were peals of thunder, loud noises, flashes of lightning, and an earthquake" (verse 5). God's judgment now begins to accelerate, sweeping closer and closer to the grand finale. The seventh seal brings the seven trumpet blasts that will bring increased suffering and destruction upon the earth. But those who are marked and sealed for the day of redemption are ready and unafraid.

For a summary of the seven seals see the chart on page 37. This is designed according to the view just presented above. If we were supposing that Christ came with the great events that end chapter 6, then the interlude on the chart would be the conclusion of what happened when the sixth seal was opened. The bottom line of the chart, the seventh-seal line, would have but one thing—silence symbolizing eternal peace (8:1).

The rest of mankind, who were not killed by these plagues, did not repent of the works of their hands nor give up worshiping demons and idols of gold and silver and bronze and stone and wood, which cannot either see or hear or walk; nor did they repent of their murders or their sorceries or their immorality or their thefts.

Revelation 9:20, 21

Revelation 8:6 — 11:19
Reading and Study Outline

I. The First Six Trumpets (8:6—9:21)

II. Intermediate Visions (10:1—11:14)
   The Sealing of Seven Thunders (10:1-7)
   The Little Scroll (10:8-11)
   The Measuring of the Temple (11:1-3)
   The Two Witnesses (11:4-14)

III. The Seventh Trumpet (11:15-19)

It's Getting Worse, Fast

The Seven Trumpets and Intermediate Visions
Revelation 8:6 – 11:19

We are in the last days, but are we getting close to the end of time? Many students of Bible prophecy are saying, "Yes," but there are still many skeptics. I remember seeing a cartoon that depicted Adam and Eve being driven from the Garden of Eden. Just outside the gate a bearded man in a long robe is carrying a sign that reads, "Repent! The end is near."

In comparison with eternity there is perhaps but a short time between creation and the end, and certainly there is even less time today. Jesus said He would come again soon (Revelation 22:20). However relative that term may have been, we know that we are much closer today to His second coming. But the time of the end remains unpredictable, although there are "prophets" who like to try their hand at pinpointing it.

In 1528 a bookbinder by the name of Hans Nut (his real name, no pun intended!) claimed that he had been sent by Christ to forewarn of His coming. According to Mr. Nut, the Lord's second coming would take place later that same year. A more recent report has been issued jointly by scientists at Harvard University and Massachusetts Institute of Technology. It concluded that a nuclear war is likely by 1984, and that an all-out, worldwide conflict is almost certain by the end of the century. As I write, this prediction remains to be tested.

If Jesus himself would not predict the time of His coming again, it

41

certainly does not seem wise for us to. "But of that day and hour no one knows," Jesus said, "not even the angels of heaven, nor the Son, but the Father only" (Matthew 24:36). Nevertheless we can see that in many ways the world situation is getting worse, fast. This is essentially the message of the seven trumpet blasts: as the end draws closer, tribulation intensifies.

The First Six Trumpets (8:6−9:21)

1. Hail and fire with blood (verse 7)

With the blast of the first trumpet there come upon the earth hail and fire mixed with blood. The hail and blood remind us of the Egyptian plagues that God worked through Moses. Again God brings His judgment upon the earth, not as an end in itself, but to move men to do His will. At the sound of this trumpet, one-third of the earth's vegetation is destroyed.

2. Fire into the sea (verses 8, 9)

The second trumpet blast is directed against the sea and sea life. Something like a mountain of fire is cast into the sea, perhaps suggesting volcanic action. Now one-third of all sea life is destroyed, including the ships on the sea.

Our local newspaper commented on an article that had appeared in the *U. S. News and World Report* titled "Is Mother Nature Going Berserk?" Some of the concerns it discussed were these:

1. "If South Pole ice melts . . . a warming earth could melt 7 million cubic miles of ice . . . raising sea level 250 feet and flooding coastal states."

2. "There are fears that earthquakes and volcanoes in the decades just ahead may create unprecedented destruction."

3. "Earthquakes are not the only concern. . . . The Cascade Range volcanoes (in the West) are brooding threats." This is a suggestion of second-trumpet activity.

3. Wormwood: the falling star (verses 10, 11)

First it is one-third of the earth, then one-third of the sea that is affected. Now one-third of the fresh waters on the earth are made bitter, unpalatable, and evidently poisonous by the falling star, which is curiously named Wormwood. In terms of current military technology, the contamination of the waters by the falling star may suggest radiation fallout. In any case, the result John sees is that "many men died."

The First Six Trumpets

Trumpet	Revelation	Place	Action	Result
1	8:7	Earth	Hail, fire, blood fall	1/3 vegetation destroyed
2	8:8, 9	Sea	Fiery Mountain cast into sea	End of 1/3 fish, ships
3	8:10, 11	Rivers	Big star falls	Pollution, death
4	8:12	Sky	Sun, moon, stars struck	Loss of light
Interlude	8:13	Midheaven	Eagle shouts	Woe, woe, woe!
5	9:1-11	Earth	Locusts sting	Torture to unsealed people
6	9:13-21	Earth	War, plagues	1/3 people killed

4. Sun, moon, and stars struck (verse 12)

With the blast of the fourth trumpet all available light sources are diminished by one-third. Days become gloomy, dimmer. Nights are blacker. Coldness sets in; crops and food supplies are affected. The fourth trumpet seems to be symbolic or prophetic of increasing evil and impending doom. The light of God's grace is going out.

Interlude: The eagle's cry (verse 13)

The first four trumpet blasts represent tribulation upon the earth added to that brought on by the opening of the first six seals. The eagle's cry is a warning that with the next three trumpet blasts tribulation will become increasingly worse: "Woe, woe, woe!" It's getting worse, fast.

5. The locusts' stings (9:1-11)

The falling star of verse 1 probably represents Satan. (Compare Luke 10:18-20.) The smoke from the pit brings darkness and delusion, and from it come the locusts who torture the unsealed. Christians (the sealed) will not be hurt by their sting (see Luke 10:18-20 again), nor will the fiery darts of Satan be able to penetrate their shields of faith (see Ephesians 6:16). On the other hand, the locusts' stings will be so severe that the unsealed will actually prefer death.

A young woman asked me to visit her father in the hospital. I found him in the psychiatric ward, a man near my own age. He was nicely dressed, and his hair was neatly combed. Only his eyes betrayed the weariness of his soul. He told me his life's story: a tragic tale of one woe upon another. Finally he exclaimed, "Why don't they just leave me alone? My life is so miserable I just want to die!" It was not an uncommon plea. For many the sting of sin and of life's tragedies becomes so unbearable that death seems preferable to life (verse 6).

Some commentators have seen in the description of the locusts (verses 7-11) a prophetic vision of war planes. They are "like horses" (much larger than locusts); they have "crowns" (cockpits); "human faces" (pilots); "hair" and "teeth" (conceivably painted designs like those of the "Flying Tigers"); "iron breastplates" (made of metal); "noise of their wings" (engines); "and their power of hurting men for five months lies in their tails" (tail gunners or bombardiers). These are interesting possibilities, although all this must be viewed as speculation, not interpretation. Before war planes were well developed, some students suggested that John saw a vision of horse-drawn artillery. The locusts that looked like horses were real horses, the human faces were faces of their riders, the crowns were the riders' helmets, the teeth were the riders' weapons, the hair like women's hair was the horses manes, and the stings in their tails were the cannon they pulled. Whatever the locusts represent, one important thing to remember is that their mission is to inflict pain and suffering, not death (verse 5). Death is yet to come.

The king of these horrid creatures is the one who brings them out of the pit (verse 11). His two names both mean *destroyer*. A third name, Satan, means *adversary*. He is the enemy of God and man, the destroyer of what is good.

6. *War and plagues (9:13-21)*

The four angels from the East are poised and ready for the exact moment when they will be released to destroy one-third of mankind. Their combined armies total an incredible two hundred million! That may seem to be an exaggerated way of referring to unnumbered masses or insurmountable odds. But a footnote to this verse in *The Living Bible* quotes an Associated Press release, dated April 24, 1964, stating that in 1961 there were "an estimated 200,000,000 armed and organized militiamen" *in China alone* (italics mine). This may be taken as a symbolic number and event in Revelation, but it can also be taken literally. The resulting three plagues destroy one-third of mankind.

What is the purpose of the sixth trumpet blast and the terrific slaughter? Perhaps the purpose of all the trumpets and of the seals is suggested by verses 20 and 21: "The rest of mankind . . . did not repent." God is intent on the salvation of the world, not its condemnation and destruction. (See John 3:16, 17.) He does not wish "that any should perish, but that all should reach repentance" (2 Peter 3:9). Tribulation is meant to be redemptive for those who will repent, but destructive for those who will not.

Intermediate Visions (10:1–11:14)

1. *The sealing of the seven thunders (10:1-7)*

The message of the seven thunders remains a mystery. "Seal up what the seven thunders have said, and do not write it down" (verse 4). At least this much is clear: Not all has been revealed. This should serve as a warning to modern-day prophets who claim to have all the pieces of the puzzle neatly put together. Some of the pieces are not even given. We must continue to put our trust in the God who reveals, not in the man who interprets, whether that be ourselves or some other.

2. The eating of the scroll (10:8-11)

This vision is like a riddle. Question: What is sweet to the taste but bitter to the stomach? Answer: the Word of God (the scroll). The good news of the gospel is sweet to those who receive it and believe. But to those who selfishly retain it for themselves it becomes bitter condemnation. Or, as some see it, the gospel taken into the life brings bitter persecution such as John was suffering. In any case, we know the gospel is given to be put to use in our daily lives and to be shared with others. So John is instructed, "You must again prophesy about many peoples and nations and tongues and kings." The revelation was his not to keep but to share. The same is true for us as well.

3. The measuring of the temple (11:1-3)

The measuring of the temple seems to indicate the boundaries of God's judgment. It is as if to say the temple is surveyed and marked off to be specially protected, "out of bounds" to the calamities of the seventh trumpet blast that is to follow soon. The temple is symbolic of the faithful Jews of the Old Testament and Christians of the New Testament (see 1 Corinthians 3:16). The outer court, the court of the Gentiles or the nations, will be subjected to a period of persecution during which the two witnesses will prophesy.

4. The two witnesses (11:4-14)

The two witnesses may represent the law and the prophets, particularly in the persons of Moses and Elijah. Some students think they are symbols of the law and the gospel, the Old Testament and the New. This may be true, but in verse 6 "power to shut the sky, that no rain may fall during the days of their prophesying" suggests Elijah the prophet (see 1 Kings 17:1), and "power over the waters to turn them into blood, and to smite the earth with every plague" suggests Moses (see Exodus 7:17—11:5). Verse 5 may refer to an event in Moses' life or in Elijah's, or both (see Leviticus 10:1, 2; Numbers 11:1, 2; 2 Kings 1:9, 10). Moses and Elijah did "stand before the Lord of the earth" (verse 4) when they appeared with Jesus at the time of His transfiguration (Matthew 17:3). The figure of olive trees and lampstands is taken from Zechariah 4.

Intermediate Visions and Seventh Trumpet

Trumpet	Revelation	Vision	Meaning
	10:1-7	Sealing seven thunders	Not all is revealed
	10:8-11	Eating the scroll	Receive and proclaim
	11:1-3	Measuring the temple	Limits of judgment
	11:4-14	The two witnesses	Moses and Elijah The law and the prophets
7	11:15-19	The seventh trumpet	Victory

In John's vision the two witnesses are killed and the people re-joice, but the witnesses are later resurrected from the dead. Israel destroyed the witnesses by arrogant rebellion. For example, see 2 Kings 17:7-18; Matthew 23:37; Acts 7:51-53. In a sense, Christ himself resurrected them to their rightful place of witness when He said,

> Think not that I have come to abolish the law and the prophets; I have come not to abolish them but to fulfill them. For truly, I say to you, till heaven and earth pass away, not an iota, not a dot, will pass from the law until all is accomplished.
> Matthew 5:17, 18

These two witnesses, the law and the prophets, still bear their testimony today (Romans 15:4). They will continue to affirm the will of God and the person of the Messiah until the end of time. The Old Testament finds its completion and fulfillment in the person of Jesus, but it must not be ignored.

The Seventh Trumpet (11:15-19)

As indicated in chapter 4, there are two ways of looking at the part of Revelation we are now considering.

First, some scholars see several groups of visions representing the same time and events. Each group or series of visions portrays the tribulations of earth and then the triumph of Heaven. One series is presented with the opening of seven seals, and ends with the glori-ous vision of the redeemed in Heaven (7:9-17). Another series then is presented with the blowing of seven trumpets. These visions present the same earthly woes in a different way, and end with the same Heavenly triumph (11:15-18). Then chapter 12 begins another series of visions.

This view is set forth briefly in the chart on the following page, where five series of visions are arranged in five parallel columns. It is supposed that each series represents the course of world history from Christ's first coming to the final judgment.

For these studies we have chosen a different view of these visions. Instead of several groups of visions all representing the same time and events, we see one continuous series. The events introduced by the seven trumpets come after those introduced by the seven seals, and the events pictured in chapter 12 and following chapters come after those introduced by the trumpets. The visions of Heavenly

The Theory of Parallel Visions

Seals 5–7	Trumpets 8–11	Dragon 12:1–15:4	Bowls 15:5–16:21	Kingdom 19:11–22:21
Christ or antichrist 6:1, 2	Scorched earth 8:7	Escape 12:1-6	Affliction 16:2	Conqueror 19:11-21
Red horse—war 6:3, 4	Scorched sea 8:8, 9	War in Heaven 12:7-12	Sea death 16:3	Satan bound 20:1-3
Black horse—famine 6:5, 6	Polluted rivers 8:10, 11	Persecution 12:13-17	Bloody rivers 16:4-7	Millennium 20:4-6
Pale horse—death 6:7, 8	Dimmed lights 8:12	Sea beast 13:1-10	Scorching heat 16:8, 9	Satan loosed 20:7-9a
Justice delayed 6:9-11	Locusts 9:1-12	Earth beast 13:11-18	Anguish 16:10, 11	Satan crushed 20:9b, 10
Disaster—Redemption 6:12—7:17	Human death 9:13-20	The redeemed 14:1-5	Call to conflict 16:12-16	Judgment 20:11-15
Silence	Rule of Christ 11:15-19	Judgment 14:6—15:4	Done! 16:17-21	Eternity 21, 22

glory and triumph are interludes inserted to encourage those in the midst of tribulation. In this view, the visions presented in parallel columns on page 49 are better arranged in a single column as follows:

The Seals (chapters 5:1—8:6)
1. White horse (6:1, 2)
2. Red horse—war (6:3, 4)
3. Black horse—famine (6:5, 6)
4. Pale horse—death (6:7, 8)
5. Justice delayed (6:9-11)
6. Disaster (6:12-17)
   Encouragement (chapter 7)
7. Introduction of trumpets (8:1-6)

The Trumpets (chapters 8:7—11:19)
1. Scorched earth (8:7)
2. Scorched sea (8:8, 9)
3. Polluted rivers (8:10, 11)
4. Dimmed lights (8:12)
5. Locusts (9:1-12)
6. Human death (9:13-20)
7. *Encouragement (11:15-19)*

The Dragon (12:1—15:4)
Escape (12:1-6)
Flashback to earlier war (12:7-12)
Persecution (12:13-17)
Sea beasts (13:1-10)
Earth beast (13:11-18)
Encouragement (chapter 14)

The Bowls (15:5—19:10)
1. Affliction (16:2)
2. Sea death (16:3)
3. Bloody rivers (16:4-6)
4. Scorching heat (16:8, 9)
5. Anguish (16:10, 11)
6. Call to conflict (16:12-16)
7. End of Babylon (16:17-21)
   Encouragement (19:1-9)

The Kingdom (19:11—22:21)
   Conqueror (19:11-21)
   Satan bound (20:1-3)
   Millennium (20:4-6)
   Satan loosed (20:7-9a)
   Satan crushed (20:9b, 10)
   Judgment (20:11-15)
   Eternity (21, 22)

The reader, of course, can choose either of these views, or perhaps select some other that seems to fit the Scriptures better. It seems to me, however, that the seventh trumpet introduces not only Revelation 11:15-18, but also the visions that follow in chapter 12 and the following chapters, including those of the seven bowls of wrath described in chapter 16. There are pictured the seven last plagues, "for with them the wrath of God is ended" (15:1).

With the blowing of the seventh trumpet the end is near, the final battle will soon be fought, but the declaration of victory has already been made. "The kingdom of the world has become the kingdom of our Lord and of his Christ, and he shall reign for ever and ever" (11:15). In Christ we are already victors, although the final battle has not yet been fought. God has revealed to us who the winner will be. All we have to do is choose which side we will be on.

The seven trumpet blasts are warning of persecution and destruction that will come upon the earth. How can you best be prepared? I have read of "Christians" (I question the Christianity of their acts) who are preparing by purchasing guns and by taking target practice. As one said, "When the holocaust begins and people try to come to us for food, they'll be met with a gun. Because if they wait until then to prepare, it will be too late."

The real preparation, however, comes through repentance. That is what God wants. After one-third of mankind is destroyed, why don't the remaining two-thirds repent? (9:20, 21). Wouldn't you? If your answer is "Yes," then do it now. As a little plaque has aptly stated, "REPENT: if you have already repented you may disregard this message." This is God's message in Revelation. Don't disregard it. If you have already repented, then you are ready to join in the victory celebration.

When the dragon saw that he had been thrown down to the earth, he pursued the woman who had borne the male child . . . and went off to make war on the rest of her offspring, on those who keep the commandments of God and bear testimony to Jesus.
Revelation 12:13, 17

Revelation 12
Reading and Study Outline

I. The Woman and the Male Child (12:1-6)
   Satan vs. Christ

II. The Battle in Heaven (12:7-12)
   Satan vs. Heaven

III. The Attack on Earth (12:13-17)
   Satan vs. Earth

Attack From Outer Space

The Woman, the Male Child, and the Deceiver
Revelation 12

On October 30, 1938, this nation came to near panic upon hearing Orson Welles' dramatic radio production of H. G. Wells' "War of the Worlds." The story was based on the fictitious announcement that the earth had been invaded by Martians. There were many frightened believers. Since then many science-fiction horror stories have been produced on radio, TV, and film. But all of them put together would not be nearly so frightening as one of God's revealed truths: the earth has indeed been invaded, by Satan and the forces of evil. We are under attack! The real danger is greater than any invented by Orson Welles.

P. T. Barnum of Barnum and Bailey Circus popularized the saying, "There is a sucker born every minute." (With our population explosion, the rate is probably much higher today!) It occurs to me that there are at least two kinds of "suckers" or dupes: the gullible and the godless.

The gullible are those Barnum spoke of and Welles frightened. They are those who overreacted to news of "The Jupiter Effect," the "scientific" prediction of doomsday on March 10, 1982, when nine planets would come into an unusually close alignment. Many other predictions preceded this same phenomenon. One that I particularly liked came, appropriately enough, from the New York Center for the Strange. They said the planetary alignment would trigger "nationwide shortages of sparkling wine, hockey pucks, gerbil cages, and soy sauce." Could be; nobody noticed.

On the other hand, the godless type of "suckers" or dupes are those who believe the ancient lie that "there is no God." Theirs is not so much a gullibility as a scientifically educated skepticism that in their minds eliminates the possibility, or at least the probability, that a personal God exists. Therefore they are disinterested in His promises and ignore His warnings. How sad and how foolish!

Revelation 12 is God's warning that we are under attack from outer space. Satan has invaded. History and experience verify it. You had better believe it.

The Woman and the Male Child (12:1-6)

The revelation that John now receives and records tells of Christ's birth, Satan's expulsion from Heaven, and his attack upon the earth. It is background material for understanding what follows: his rise to earthly power and his ultimate and final defeat.

The woman, at first, is Israel, who gives birth to the Messiah. Later (verse 17) she seems to be the community of the faithful, whose offspring are both Jews and Christians who now are "the Israel of God" (Galatians 6:16). The twelve stars in her crown represent the twelve tribes, Israel's "crowning glory," and are reminiscent of Joseph's dream (Genesis 37:9). The stars of that dream represented the fathers of Israel's tribes.

Satan is portrayed as a dragon (fierce), red (bloodthirsty), with seven heads (extremely wise and cunning), and ten horns (immensely powerful). The diadems represent the power of authority. His strength is demonstrated when his tail sweeps down one-third of the stars. Can these represent his angels? (See 2 Peter 2:4 and Jude 6.) Satan awaits the birth of the male child in order to destroy Him, perhaps reflecting the role of Herod at the birth of Christ.

The child is easily identified as the Christ, the "one who is to rule all the nations with a rod of iron." (See Revelation 19:15.) The story moves immediately from His birth to His ascension (verse 5), which tells us that the dragon was ineffective in his efforts to destroy Him. The woman is a fugitive for 1260 days (three and a half years), a period of tribulation. But during this time she has the special protection and provision of God (verse 6). (The story will resume at this point in verse 13. Verses 7 through 12 are a flashback telling us how Satan got to this earth in the first place.)

This vision reminds of a great truth. It reminded John and the early

The Woman and the Male Child
Revelation 12:1-6

Vision	Description	Meaning	Scriptures
Woman (verses 1, 2)	Sun, moon, stars Pregnant	Israel	Genesis 37:9, 10
Dragon (verses 3, 4)	7 heads, 10 horns Destruction tail	Satan	Revelation 12:9
Child (verse 5)	Ruler Ascended	Christ	Psalm 2:7-9 Revelation 19:15
Flight (verse 6)	Wilderness 1260 days	Persecution	Revelation 12:13-16

church, who were suffering tribulation and persecution (see Revelation 1:9 and John 16:33). It is a reminder to us today as well. It tells us that *Satan did not and could not defeat Christ*. He could not and did not thwart God's plan in Christ to redeem mankind. Therefore those who are "in Christ" have nothing to fear.

The Battle in Heaven (12:7-12)

Long ago, before Christ was born, there was a battle in Heaven. It was between Michael and his angels and Satan and his angels. The latter were defeated and were eternally banished from Heaven (verse 9).

Christ actually witnessed Satan's fall. Perhaps He referred to it when He said, "I saw Satan fall like lightning from heaven" (Luke 10:18). Evidently this was something He witnessed before He came to earth, even before the beginning of time, since Satan has been on this earth from the start of man's history. It was he, that "ancient serpent," who was with Adam and Eve in the garden, tempting them to disobey God as he himself had done.

This vision reveals how Satan came to be on the earth, and it provides us with a warning: "But woe to you, O earth and sea, for the devil has come down to you in great wrath, because he knows that his time is short!" (verse 12). Angrily and hurriedly Satan is tempting all whom he can to join him in his condemnation and banishment from Heaven. He is a fearsome opponent, and the warning is strong and clear: "Be sober, be watchful. Your adversary the devil prowls around like a roaring lion, seeking some one to devour" (1 Peter 5:8).

However, the means for defeating Satan are available to us earthlings, too. Victory is assured "by the blood of the Lamb"—that is, by Jesus' death on the cross—and "by the word of their testimony, for they loved not their lives even unto death" (verse 11)—that is, by continuing throughout our lives as His faithful witnesses. "Be faithful unto death, and I will give you the crown of life" (Revelation 2:10). We have an awesome adversary, but our Ally is greater still.

The Attack on Earth (12:13-17)

The woman, Israel, is the mother of the Messiah and therefore of the church: she is the symbol of all God's redeemed people. Having lost the battle in Heaven, Satan now directs his attack against her. But God provides her with refuge and protection. Indeed, Jesus has personally given His church this assurance: "On this rock I will build my church, and the powers of death shall not prevail against it" (Matthew 16:18). We are under His divine care. The devil cannot destroy us unless we ourselves leave our place of refuge.

Certainly natural calamities such as a flood (verse 15) cannot destroy the church of Christ. This particular flood, however, comes from Satan's mouth. It is a flood of lies and temptations and trials meant to lure the faithful away from the refuge of the church and into the bondage of sin. But even this overwhelming flood can be rendered ineffective. "No temptation has overtaken you that is not common to man. God is faithful, and he will not let you be tempted beyond your strength, but with the temptation will also provide the way of escape, that you may be able to endure it" (1 Corinthians 10:13).

The dragon's anger is now directed specifically against the woman's offspring who are believers, "those who keep the commandments of God and bear testimony to Jesus" (verse 17). Satan's attack is not really against the whole earth, for there are many who are already on his side and in his bondage. Rather, his attack is aimed at the church, at everyone who is an obedient believer.

This means there is a spiritual battle of vast dimensions going on right now for your allegiance—for your soul. If you are not aware of this conflict or feel it does not involve you, be careful! Some people are in the bondage of sin and do not realize it. Satan does not have to do battle with those who are already on his side. On the other hand, if you have decided to follow Jesus and you are trying daily to live for Him, then you know you have a real battle on your hands. But God will equip you for the battle (see Ephesians 6:10-18) and He "gives us the victory through our Lord Jesus Christ" (1 Corinthians 15:57). So give thanks.

Satan is angry and he is on the attack. But his defeat is guaranteed. In fact, it was accomplished when Jesus Christ died on the cross. But he is not defeated in your life until you personally accept Jesus as your Savior and begin to live for Him. You can choose good or evil, righteousness or sin, God or Satan. God's plea through Jesus is that you will use your freedom to choose righteousness and life. "For the wages of sin is death, but the free gift of God is eternal life in Christ Jesus our Lord" (Romans 6:23).

This calls for wisdom: let him who has understanding reckon the number of the beast, for it is a human number, its number is six hundred and sixty-six.
Revelation 13:18

Revelation 13, 14
Reading and Study Outline

"666"

Two Beasts, the Mark, and a Call to Endurance
Revelation 13, 14

A cute and clever story has been told about two little boys who were walking home one Sunday after church. One of them asked the other, "Who do you think the devil really is?" Thoughtfully his friend replied, "Well, you know how Santa Claus turned out. He's probably just your dad!"

A young woman recently told me a quite different kind of story. She works in a local grocery store as a checkout clerk. She was startled and somewhat shaken when she looked up at a young man she was checking out and saw clearly marked on his forehead the numbers "666." "I really didn't know what to say or do," she told me. "I'm afraid I just stared."

Was it just another silly, foolish fad this young man was participating in? Perhaps. But witches' covens, Satan worship, and "666" cultism are on the rise. One thing is certain—Satan is no joke! God obviously takes him seriously in Revelation, chapters 13 and 14, and is prepared to deal harshly with both Satan and those who accept his mark.

The Sea Beast (13:1-10)
The meaning of the imagery used for the "beast rising out of the sea" can be found in Revelation 17. The sea represents the nations (17:15). The ten horns are ten kings (17:12), and the seven heads are

seven mountains (17:9) and also seven kings (17:10). The comparison in 13:2 with three animals may suggest that this beast is characterized by some of their traits: swift and cunning like a leopard, strong and powerful like a bear, ferocious and destructive like a lion. (Compare Daniel 7:1-7.) The beast's "power and his throne and great authority" (Revelation 13:2) are all from the dragon. They are not his own.

He seems to be invincible: "Who is like the beast, and who can fight against it?" (verse 4). This reputation may have come from the apparent demise and resuscitation of one of its heads, possibly representing the fall and rise of a king or kingdom (verse 3). The sea beast is blasphemous and has great authority, although it is limited to forty-two months (verses 5, 6). He is able to conquer the saints (verse 7), but this must be understood to be only a physical conquest, since "we are more than conquerors through him who loved us" (Romans 8:37). All worship the beast except the saints (verse 8). The proper response to his onslaught is to accept captivity if it comes, but not to take up weapons: that is suicidal (verse 10). Our victory over Satan and his allies must be won on the spiritual front.

The multiple heads of the sea beast suggest that he is more than an individual, or a single king or kingdom. The symbolism seems to represent a powerful, earthly, diabolical government or political system. It is a government that opposes God, serves Satan, fosters evil. And it persecutes the church. Rome, Germany, Russia, and others have at times seemed to fit this category, and who knows what antichrists may be in the future?

A board member of International Aid was recently ordered out of Romania for associating with the "wrong people": that is, Christians. He accused the secret police there of persecuting Christians who were guilty of nothing more than practicing their faith. He reported that the weapons used by the communist government there in its anti-Christian program included arrests, beatings, mind-altering drugs, confinement in mental institutions, loss of jobs, refusal to grant food coupons, and even murder. It looks as if the sea beast is hard at work!

What should a Christian do in a case like this? Endure and keep the faith (verse 10). Go to captivity if that becomes necessary, but do not retaliate with physical violence. And never worship the beast or submit spiritually to Satan, even if refusing means death. That is the meaning of being faithful *unto death:* that is, to the point of dying in order to remain true to God.

The Earth Beast (13:11-17)

The chief characteristic of the earth beast is its deceitfulness: "It deceives those who dwell on earth" (verse 14). It has the appearance of a lamb (Christ-like), but speaks like a dragon (Satan-like) (verse 11). It uses the authority of the first beast to force earth's inhabitants to worship him (the first beast) (verse 12). Failure to do so results in death (verse 15). It is the earth beast who forces everyone "to be marked on the right hand or the forehead" (verse 16). The mark can be either the beast's name or his number, and without it one will suffer economic boycott (verse 17). This will mean destitution, exposure, starvation, and death.

The second beast seems to be a powerful earthly political leader. He uses deception, trying to look like a lamb (verse 11). But he also uses the political and military power of the first beast, a godless government, to force people away from God and into the service of Satan. How quickly and clearly the early Christians reading the book of Revelation would identify Rome as the first beast and the emperor (Domitian or perhaps Nero) as the second beast, especially once they had read the number of his name! (verse 18).

Christians reading this book today should be as quick to hear and to heed God's warning. God teaches us to obey government and those who are in authority. But if government or political or military leaders begin to demand that we deny God and serve Satan, then it is better to suffer hunger, prison, and death. Do not take the mark and identify yourself as a servant of Satan. Maintain your identity as a servant of God at all costs!

The Mark of the Beast (13:18)

"This calls for wisdom: let him who has understanding reckon the number of the beast, for it is a human number, its number is six hundred and sixty six" (verse 18). Wisdom, indeed! How would the early Christians understand this number, and how should we? There are numerous possibilities.

Many alphabets, including the Hebrew, Greek, and Latin, have numerical values assigned to some or all of the letters. The best known to us today are the Roman numerals (Latin letters) where I is 1, V is 5, X is 10, L is 50, C is 100, and M is 1,000. In Hebrew, the title of Nero Caesar was *Neron Kaiser* (Nrvn Ksr) and had—you guessed it—the numerical value of 666. (See the chart on page 63.) This would have been a possible interpretation by Hebrews living in John's day.

This same system, however, has been used to identify other possible antichrists, both then and later. At one time, for example, it was noted that one of the titles for the Pope was the Vicar of God's Son. In Latin this is *Vicarius Filii Dei,* the sum total of the numerical value of these letters being 666. (This ignores letters that are not used as numbers.) A seminary student about the time of World War II figured out that if you assign numbers to our alphabet (making A represent 100, B represent 101, and so on), then the numerical value of the letters in the name *Hitler* adds up to 666. Similar processes have been used to "prove" that 666 stands for VISA, computer, Henry Kissinger, and a number of United States Presidents!

Another popular interpretation is that 666 is a symbolic rather than a literal number, meaning that three groups having six numbers each are combined in an eighteen-digit number. Your individual identifying "mark" could then be construed as follows: world code number (666), national code number (a three-digit number for the United States might be, for example, 110), regional code number (you already have one assigned by the postal system; mine is 672), plus your social security number of nine digits. This is purely conjecture, of course, but it is quite plausible.

There is yet another symbolic interpretation of the number. In Hebrew thought, the number seven stood for perfection. Six, being less than seven, was therefore less than perfect: it stood for evil. Then 666 may be taken to represent absolute evil rather than a person. In the Sibylline Oracles written in early Christian times, the number 888 was used to represent Jesus. In fact, the numerical value of the Greek letters in the name *Jesus* does add up to 888. The symbolism then may be as follows: 666—absolute evil; 777—absolute perfection; 888—Jesus, "beyond perfection."

Let's just suppose we are dealing with a literal number, either 666 or an eighteen-digit number. (Remember, however, the mark of the beast could be either his number or his name, according to verse 17.) Who in his right mind would be willing to accept such a number on his hand or forehead? Remember the young man I told you about; he already has. And you might too, if you were not aware of what this would mean. This beast has ways of deceiving those who dwell on earth (Revelation 13:14).

Here is how you or I might accept such a mark. We may be fast becoming a moneyless society. The "cash cards" the banks issue are one evidence of this. Computer transactions are increasingly common. The day may come when the only way to do business, to buy

Who Is 666?

Nero Caesar	The Pope	Hitler
Hebrew	*Latin*	*English*

נ ר ז נ קסר		VICARIUS		Let A = 100	
(NRVN KSR)		FILII		B = 101	
		DEI		C = 102	
				etc.	
		(Vicar of the Son of God)			
נ	50	V	5	H	107
ר	200	I	1	I	108
ז	6	C	100	T	119
נ	50	A	0	L	111
		R	0	E	104
ק	100	I	1	R	117
ס	60	U	5		666
ר	200	S	0		
	666				
		F	0		
		I	1		
		L	50		
		I	1		
		I	1		
		D	500		
		E	0		
		I	1		
			666		

and sell, will be through the use of a money card. But what if your card were lost or stolen? You would lose everything.

For security's sake you could have your number painlessly and permanently tatooed onto the back of your right hand (so that everyone would wear it in the same place) or on your forehead (amputees would need this option). Then when you bought groceries, after the clerk had passed the coded containers over the scanner, you would simply pass your hand over the scanner and the transaction would be complete! What could be more simple or more convenient?

The actual mark of the beast, of course, may have absolutely nothing to do with what is suggested above. This is simply an illustration to show that a literal mark is feasible. Could such a mark be the "mark of the beast"? That would depend, I suppose, on its being used in such a manner as to require a denial of faith. Satan is subtle; the beast is deceptive; we must be wise.

Who is the antichrist and how is he identified? The Bible tells us.

> Children, it is the last hour; and as you have heard that antichrist is coming, so now *many* antichrists have come; therefore we know that it is the last hour. . . . Who is the liar but he who denies that Jesus is the Christ? This is the antichrist, he who denies the Father and the Son.
>
> 1 John 2:18, 22

Be careful that you do not focus on the number and on the mechanics of the mark so much that you miss the message. Many Christians today seem to fear the mark and its physical consequences more than they fear sin and its eternal consequences (see Luke 12:4, 5 and Revelation 14:9-11). Whatever else the mark of the beast may mean or be it is this: *sin*. But sin can be conquered, and so can "the beast and its image and the number of its name" (read Revelation 15:2). Here is the secret of success when it comes to the mark, or to the beast, or to sin: "Submit yourselves therefore to God. Resist the devil and he will flee from you" (James 4:7).

The Call to Endurance (14:1-13)
The 144,000 (the redeemed, verse 3) are also marked. As sin is the identifying mark of those who are outside of Christ, the identifying mark of the Christian is the Holy Spirit, spoken of elsewhere as a "seal" (Ephesians 1:13, 14). They are not literally male virgins (verse

4). Rather, this further identifies them as the church, which is pure and undefiled, spotless and without blemish (see 2 Corinthians 11:2; Ephesians 5:25-27).

John now envisions three angels, each having an announcement to make. The first angel announces, "Judgment *has* come" (verses 6, 7). This is it! We are now in the seventh trumpet of the seventh seal, about to begin the seven-bowl judgments of God's wrath: "for with them the wrath of God is ended" (15:1).

The second angel announces, "Babylon is fallen" (verse 8). The details of the fall of Babylon are revealed in chapters 17 through 19, but it is prophesied here as an accomplished fact. The entire system of evil, all the forces of Satan, are doomed.

The third angel announces, "The marked shall be tormented forever" (verses 9-11). The wine of God's wrath is unmixed, undiluted, full strength. There will be no reprieve from this suffering: "the smoke of their torment goes up for ever and ever" (verse 11).

The purpose of these angelic announcements is stated in verse 12. It is a call to endurance. The church will suffer tribulation, but those who endure will receive the reward of God's personal blessing (verse 13).

The Sickle and the Winepress (14:14-20)

To encourage God's people to endure, the Lord gave John a vision of the final harvest. Part of it belongs to Jesus, the "one like a son of man, with a golden crown on his head" (verse 14). He swings His sickle and reaps earth's harvest. Then an angel swings another sickle and gathers the grapes that are thrown into the winepress of God's wrath: that is, they are subjected to His wrath and punishment. This is the harvest of the wicked who are doomed to eternal destruction. One of the primary themes of Revelation has again been stated: the righteous will be rewarded and the wicked will be punished.

God has revealed to us the enemy: the dragon, the sea beast, the earth beast, and their followers. Or, as Paul states plainly in Ephesians 6:10-12, our enemy is the devil, principalities and powers, world rulers of darkness, spiritual hosts of wickedness. The choice is clear-cut: either you choose sin, thereby taking the mark of the beast, or you choose the way of righteousness and follow Jesus, thereby taking His mark, the Holy Spirit. For the person who is in Christ, marked and sealed by the Holy Spirit, 666 with all that it represents is a paper tiger.

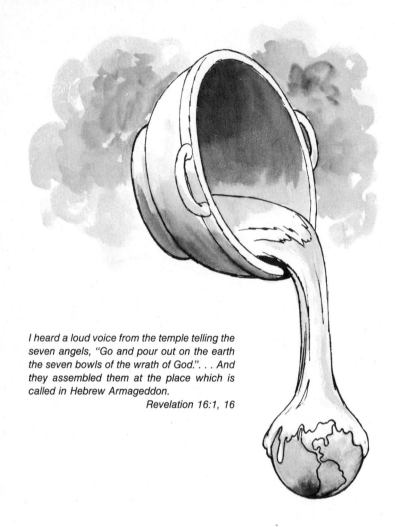

*I heard a loud voice from the temple telling the
seven angels, "Go and pour out on the earth
the seven bowls of the wrath of God.". . . And
they assembled them at the place which is
called in Hebrew Armageddon.*

Revelation 16:1, 16

Revelation 15, 16
Reading and Study Outline

I. Prelude to the Seven Bowl Judgments (15:1-8)

II. The Seven Bowl Judgments (16:1-21)

III. Conclusion: The Battle of Armageddon

The Great Tribulation

The Seven Bowl Judgments
Revelation 15, 16

Are you ready for the end? Because this is it! With the emptying of the seventh and last bowl of judgment God will announce, "It is done!" (16:17).

A Sunday-school teacher was attempting to dramatize the end of time for her children. "There will be lightning, hail, earthquakes, darkness, death, and destruction," she explained. One youngster asked hopefully, "Does that mean we will get out of school?" That's one way of putting it. School will be over. Church will be over. History will be over.

We are now living in the last days. We are now experiencing tribulation. But as the time draws closer for Jesus to return to earth, tribulation evidently will intensify until finally earth and all its inhabitants will be destroyed. Then God's justice will be enacted; then eternity will begin.

The seven bowl judgments represent the time of this great, intense tribulation. They come as our final warning from God. We had better pay attention.

Prelude to the Seven Bowl Judgments (15:1-8)
These seven plagues will complete God's wrath against the earth (verse 1). These are announced as the last of God's judgments. This is the end.

John now sees a beautiful, Heavenly scene (verse 2), and two questions are answered for us. First, "Can the beast and his number be conquered?" Yes, John sees the conquerors in this vision. Second, "Where are the dead?" Those who have died in the Lord, the conquerors, are already with Him, harps in hand, singing Moses' song.

God's judgments may seem to be extreme, harsh, and unfair. But Moses' song, sung by the saints, reminds us that He is just: "Just and true are thy ways" (verse 3). It declares also that He is holy: "For thou alone art holy" (verse 4). Even when life seems to be most unfair, God is worthy of our worship.

It is interesting to note that the angels from the temple, God's messengers, are not dressed for battle. The bright linen and golden girdles (verse 6) are priestly attire. Why? Because the upcoming final battle will be no battle at all, no contest. There will be no recourse for the enemies of God. His judgment cannot be contested. He is simply going to "dish it out," or rather, in this case, "bowl it out."

The angels now are prepared to pour out God's wrath upon the earth. Their bowls are filled with His wrath (verse 7), and smoke fills the temple so that the glory of God is hidden from view (verse 8). It is as if God's wrath and judgments keep us from seeing Him clearly.

"In the world you have tribulation," Jesus said (John 16:33). Sufferings, heartaches, and tragedies may lead us to wonder, "Is God really there?" Or we may ask, "If God is love, how can this be?" But someday the smoke will clear and we will see God face to face. Then we will clearly understand His justice and His discipline. In the meantime we must trust, obey, and worship Him. God *is* in His holy temple.

The Seven Bowl Judgments (16:1-21)

The command is now given: "Go and pour out on the earth the seven bowls of the wrath of God" (verse 1). It is spoken only once to all seven angels, suggesting that what happens now comes in quick succession, without pause, interlude, rest, or relief. (For an outline of the place, action, and result of the seven bowl judgements see the chart on page 71.)

1. Upon the earth (verse 2)

The first bowl of wrath is poured out upon the earth. It is not, however, an indiscriminate judgment upon all men. The foul and evil sores come specifically on those "who bore the mark of the beast and worshiped its image." The implication is that the faithful servants of the Lord are also on the earth, but they are untouched by this plague.

2. Into the sea (verse 3)

The second bowl is poured into the sea, turning it to blood. Or at least it becomes "*like* the blood of a dead man." The result is the annihilation of all sea life. This stands in stark contrast to the second trumpet blast, which resulted in the destruction of only one-third of all the sea life. Total destruction now comes to the sea. "Every living thing died."

3. Into the rivers (verses 4-7)

Next in his vision John sees the third bowl being poured into the fresh water supplies upon the earth: the rivers, streams, and springs. These all turn to blood. Now there is no water to drink. What cruel and unusual punishment this seems to be! But it does not seem unjust when you recall the cry of the martyred saints whose blood has been spilled by unholy men (Revelation 6:9-11). Wicked and bloodthirsty men have craved blood; now they are given blood to drink. "Vengeance is mine, I will repay, says the Lord" (Romans 12:19).

As if in response to an anticipated cry of outrage and injustice, the angel of water declares God's judgment to be just: "It is their due!" Now those who are around the altar respond with enthusiasm, as if cheering Him on: "Yea, Lord God the Almighty, true and just are thy judgments!"

4. Upon the sun (verses 8, 9)

The fourth bowl of judgment is poured out on the sun, magnifying its heat so that men are scorched by the fierce heat. Severe sunburn, blisters, and increased suffering are now added to the thirst caused by the third bowl. Apparently even at this stage of human history, the time of God's final outpouring of wrath and judgment upon the earth, it is not too late to repent. But God is cursed instead, "and they did not repent and give him glory."

5. Upon the throne of the beast (verses 10, 11)

The effect of the fifth bowl is darkness upon the earth. Consequently men curse God and still do not repent. The darkness seems only to intensify the pain, suffering, and anguish.

I remember as a child visiting the Carlsbad Caverns in New Mexico with my parents. At a certain point down in the depths of the cave the guide had us sit down on concrete benches. Then, after he had warned us, all the lights were turned off. I have never experienced such total blackness in my life. My eyes strained toward the outermost reaches of the cavern for some glimmer of gray, some form or outline, but none was there.

For a moment it seemed that we were suspended in the midst of this blackness, and that if I were to fall, I might fall in any direction. I clutched the bench tightly. My heart beat faster. I felt lost, alone, and afraid, although my shoulder was pressed hard against my mother's side.

When the lights came back on I felt very relieved, if a bit foolish. Nothing had changed except for the light—wonderful, beautiful light! Afraid of the dark? You bet I was!

It is easy to understand why darkness produces anxiety and causes anguish. If there are hazards they become much more dangerous in the darkness. Enemies become more fearsome, for without sight you are left virtually defenseless. You may become lost whether you move or remain immobile. Darkness holds the power to produce fear, confusion, lostness, panic, immobility, loneliness, anxiety, and anguish. Such is the judgment of the fifth bowl.

6. *Upon the Euphrates (verses 12-16)*

The pouring out of the sixth bowl of God's wrath causes the waters of the Euphrates River to dry up. Why water and not blood? (See verse 4.) Simply because this is the way John saw it in the vision that was given to him. This is another vision, not the same one in which the water turned to blood. The significance lies in what this symbolizes. It is "to prepare the way for the kings from the east."

This bowl also signals the assembling of those who would do battle against God Almighty. The unholy trinity—the dragon, the beast, and the false prophet—sent forth the spirits to call the kings of the whole world to battle. The place for their assembly is Armageddon.

Verse 15 seems to be an aside (placed in parentheses in some translations), intended for John's readers, the Christian community. "Don't worry about all these hordes of evil," John seems to be saying. "Just stay spiritually alert and properly clothed (in the white robes of righteousness) and you'll be okay. Remember, Jesus is coming soon to take care of you, *and* them."

70

The Seven Bowl Judgments
Revelation 16:1-21

Bowl	Place	Action	Result
1 (verse 2)	Earth	Foul and evil sores	Suffering
2 (verse 3)	Sea	Sea became like blood	Death
3 (verses 4-7)	Rivers	Water became blood	Blood to drink
4 (verses 8, 9)	Sun	Men were scorched	Cursing without repentance
5 (verses 10, 11)	Throne of the beast	Kingdom was in darkness	Anguish without repentance
6 (verses 12-16)	Euphrates River	Water was dried up	Assembly for battle
7 (verses 17-21)	Air	Lightning, earthquake, hail	Babylon punished, pain and cursing

Why would anyone enter into this alliance to do battle against God? How foolish! How ignorant! How deceived they must be! There is no chance for victory. None at all. Yet everyone who sins and does not repent and turn to God makes exactly the same foolish, eternally damning mistake. That's what this vision is all about. To the wicked God says, "Repent or perish." To the church He says, "Stay ready and don't worry."

7. Into the air (verses 17-21)

The seventh bowl is poured into the air, and the act is accompanied by the shout of the victor, "It is done!" A great cataclysmic upheaval follows, which affects the whole earth and the men upon the earth. But it is especially directed against Babylon, "to make her drain the cup of the fury of his wrath." The fall of Babylon is elaborated on in the following chapters of Revelation (17—20). Men curse God for the hail, again indicating that they deserve the punishment they are receiving. They have had every chance to repent, but they choose to defy God and shout curses.

Conclusion: The Battle of Armageddon

Armageddon is generally identified as Megiddo, which is located in the plain of Esdraelon. That plain lies across the border of the areas known as Galilee and Samaria in New Testament times. Will the kings of earth, summoned by spirits of evil, literally gather there for battle "on the great day of God the Almighty"? Many students think they will.

As we have noted several times, some students think Revelation presents several groups of visions that picture the same times and events in different ways, each group ending with the victory of Christ and the joy of His people in Heaven. According to that view, the kings from the east (16:12) may be the four angels who will kill a third of mankind (9:13-15). It is easy to imagine that the communist giants, China and the Soviet Union, may sometime patch up their differences and become allies. It is not impossible that they will take over Japan and India. If that happens, it will not be surprising if the four bring an army of "twice ten thousand times ten thousand" (9:16) to take possession of the Mid-east oil fields. Then the free world may mobilize to meet these powers from the east. The plain of Esdraelon may be the scene of confrontations—and somebody may unleash nuclear weapons capable of destroying a third of mankind (9:15).

Of course this speculation is just that—speculation and nothing more. Jesus may come and end earth's history tomorrow, or even today. Or the world may stand for a thousand years and the communist giants pass into oblivion before the final bowls of God's wrath are poured out.

What seems certain is an Armageddon greater than one brought on by twice ten thousand times ten thousand troops. The ongoing battle between evil and righteousness will come to its climax and Jesus will win, though the battlefield is not to be pinpointed on a map of the world. The Lord's battle is spiritual, and His sword is the word of God that proceeds from His mouth (1:16; 19:15). With this word He will "smite the nations" and establish His rule for eternity.

If we regard Armageddon as a symbol of this spiritual conflict, that does not mean the conflict is unreal. It is more real and more meaningful than any clash of armies, even one involving twice ten thousand times ten thousand. If literal war that kills a third of mankind seems frightening, you must understand that the spiritual warfare is terrible beyond description. I am sure that Heaven is more wonderful than the human mind can comprehend, and Hell is more horrible.

In this spiritual conflict your eternal soul is at stake. Now is the time to choose your side. You can assemble with the wicked at Armageddon to suffer the wrath of God, or you can repent and enjoy eternal life with the saints and the Lord.

*Babylon the great,
mother of harlots
and of earth's abominations.
Revelation 17:5*

Revelation 17, 18
Reading and Study Outline

The Harlot

The Harlot, the Beast, and the Fall of Babylon
Revelation 17, 18

On the Kansas frontier they were called "soiled doves." History records, however, that they were hardly glamour queens with hearts of gold, as movies and magazines today often portray prostitutes. For the most part they were homely, dirty, and diseased: and they sported such names as Squirrel-tooth Alice, Jake-leg Nell, Crooked-nose Emma, and Latch-eye Kate.

People jokingly refer to "the world's oldest profession" and "the ladies of the night" as if their illegal and sinful activity were somehow deserving of respect. Prostitution is expressly against the will of God. It is associated with organized crime, drugs, disease, divorce, blackmail, and murder. What a perfect symbol for the alluring, deceptive, destructive power of sin—the harlot!

The Mother of Harlots (17:1-6)

The woman John sees in this vision is beautifully and richly dressed. I imagine her to be very attractive and sexually appealing. But there are four things mentioned here that reveal her true character to us.

First, the scarlet beast on which she rides is none other than the sea beast, that ungodly, diabolical system of evil that serves the dragon (Satan) and leads men to worship him. (Compare 17:3 and 13:1.)

Second, the golden cup she holds is "full of abominations and the impurities of her fornication" (verse 4). She may be beautiful to look at, but the activities she participates in are repulsive and sickening.

Third, there is the name clearly displayed on her forehead for all to see: "Babylon the great, mother of harlots and of earth's abominations" (verse 5).

Fourth, she is "drunk with the blood of the saints" (verse 6). She is the bloodthirsty archenemy of God's people, hardly an attractive lady!

God's revelation here is very clear. The great Babylon against which He directs His wrath (16:19) and this harlot are one and the same: the system of evil by which Satan lures the unwary into an illicit, adulterous relationship with sin. Satan's purpose and the harlot's purpose are one: to tempt us into "playing the harlot" as Israel did. (Read Jeremiah 3:6-10.) On these grounds God divorced Israel.

God reveals this to us so that we will not be taken in by sin's beauty, wealth, and power. Sin's golden cup has all the allurement of drugs, alcohol, embezzlement, luxury, prestige, or a sexual affair. To drink from this cup, whatever the sin, is to partake of impurities, abominations, disease, and death. It is to become drunk (verse 2), spiritually drunk, losing control of your senses and possession of your soul. Beware the harlot!

The Seven Heads and the Ten Horns (17:7-14)

John marvels at this harlot (verse 6) but the angel admonishes him for it (verse 7). In case John (or we) has not yet "got the picture," the angel proceeds to show him more of the gory details of her grotesquerie.

Verse 8 sounds like a riddle: "Was . . . is not . . . is to ascend . . . and go to perdition." In Revelation 13 the beast appears as an ally of the dragon, Satan; but here in Revelation 17 the distinction seems to fade and the beast is identified with Satan himself. He was powerful from the beginning of the world; he was defeated by the death of Christ, and so in a sense he now is not; he will ascend from the bottomless pit but finally will be cast into perdition, destruction, eternal damnation (Revelation 20:1-3, 7-10).

The seven heads are seven mountains and seven kings (verses 9, 10). For the early Christians this probably pointed to Rome, symbol of godless government and antichrist sentiment and activity. Rome was built on seven hills, and the seven kings may have been Roman emperors. The beast himself is integral to this whole system (verse

The Harlot

Revelation 17:1-18

Vision	Identity	Meaning
Harlot (verse 1)	The great city, Babylon 17:5, 18	Sin, abominations, unfaithfulness
Waters (verse 1)	People, multitudes, nations, tongues 17:15	Earth's inhabitants
Beast (verse 3)	The sea beast 13:1	Diabolical government
Seven heads (verse 3)	Mountains and kings 17:9, 10	Rome and other rulers
Ten horns (verse 3)	Kings 17:12	Earthly rulers
Great City (verse 18)	Babylon, mother of harlots 17:4, 5	The system of evil on earth

11), but remember, he will be defeated and "go to perdition." He is powerful but doomed.

The ten horns are ten kings or kingdoms who were yet to come when John received this revelation. They will rule briefly ("for one hour"—verse 12); they will be similar in purpose ("of one mind"—verse 13); and they will be subservient to the beast (verse 13). All of them will make war on the Lamb, but they will, of course, be conquered (verse 14).

Modern-day "prophets" have multiplied interpretations pointing out various individuals, rulers, and nations that may be among the ten. To review all these interpretations would really be pointless. Perhaps many of them are right. Perhaps all the godless governments in the world are symbolized by the beast with his multiple heads and horns.

Sometimes we get so caught up in the symbols of Revelation that we forget they are vehicles of a revealed message, not a concealed one. This vision was a warning to the early Christians, and it is a warning to Christians of every age, to avoid the harlot of sin and all those who are in alliance with her or serve her purpose, whether they be individuals, rulers, or governments.

This grotesque beast with seven heads and ten horns cannot succeed; Christ will conquer it. Don't be deceived into thinking that sin, any sin, is okay, or that evil will somehow get you ahead. You just can't win by telling lies, or disobeying your parents, or cheating on your husband or wife, or ignoring the fellowship of the church, or by any act of disobedience to God's will. Harlotry is a real loser, as this vision next reveals.

The Destruction of the Harlot (17:15-18)

Who rules whom? The harlot has the beast in harness. She rides and controls him at will, or so it seems. Then suddenly, without warning, the beast turns against the harlot and destroys her.

How can this be, since the harlot and the beast both represent, in some aspects, sin? It is sin against sin. It is a kingdom divided against itself, and it cannot stand. Evil is self-destructive. The final result is that the system of evil is destroyed according to God's plan. Even the wicked unwittingly and unintentionally serve God's purposes.

You may think that you are in control of your sins—drinking, using drugs, lying, lusting—but sin cannot be controlled by man. If you persist in playing the role of the harlot by being unfaithful to God's will, then someday that beast that has served you and perhaps given you pleasure will turn on you and destroy you. And that destruction will be spiritual and eternal.

The Epilogue (18:1-24)

The story has been told. Happy, carefree, prosperous, pleasurable, wicked Babylon the great has been reduced to ashes, suffering, and death. The epilogue is now given, telling of the lament of her lovers and the rejoicing of the righteous.

It also contains this warning: "Come out of her, my people, lest you take part in her sins, lest you share in her plagues" (verse 4). You must choose to leave this wicked city while you can, before it is too late. It is by repentance, not rapture, that you will avoid her plagues. But where shall we flee? In faith we flee to Christ, to the holy city, the new Jerusalem that He is preparing for His own. He is coming soon.

And the angel said to me, "Write this: Blessed are those who are invited to the marriage supper of the Lamb."
Revelation 19:9

Revelation 19
Reading and Study Outline

I. The Marriage Supper and the Hallelujah Chorus (19:1-10)

II. The White Horse and the King of Kings (19:11-16)

III. The Great Supper and the Lake of Fire (19:17-21)

The King Is Coming

The Marriage Supper and the Great Supper
Revelation 19

A joke has been making the rounds recently claiming that Jesus is definitely planning to return to earth a little later this year. (That part, of course, may not be a joke!) He has sent each of His faithful followers a letter so they will know what to expect. Do you know what the letter says? No? You mean you didn't get a letter?

It is no joke that Jesus is coming again, soon. God has already issued invitations and warnings to all people, in His Son, by His Word, and through His church. Are you ready?

Actually there are two different invitations. God has invited you to the marriage supper of the Lamb. The other invitation, if you want to call it that, is to the great supper. These are by no means the same. At the first supper you will enjoy a great feast. At the second supper you *are* the feast. Be careful.

Marriage Supper and Hallelujah Chorus (19:1-10)

There is singing and rejoicing in Heaven in the vision John now sees. The great harlot has been justly judged, the saints have been avenged, and "the smoke from her goes up for ever and ever!" (verses 1-3). Evil has come to an end, and the celebration is about to begin. "Let us rejoice and exult and give him the glory, for the marriage of the Lamb has come, and his Bride has made herself ready" (verse 7).

The Bride is the church, beautifully and properly attired (Ephesians 5:25-27). Jesus told a parable comparing the kingdom of Heaven to a marriage feast that a king gave for his son (Matthew 22:2-14). One guest, you may remember, came improperly attired and was cast out into the darkness. We don't want anything like that to happen to us.

What should the guests, or the bride, wear? "Fine linen, bright and pure . . . the righteous deeds of the saints" (verse 8). How can this be? Isaiah has taught us that our righteous deeds are like "filthy rags" or "a polluted garment" (Isaiah 64:6). That is true, without Christ. But with Jesus as our Savior we are forgiven and cleansed. By His blood our righteous deeds are made acceptable, white as snow. In other words, you are properly dressed and ready for Heaven only by a combination of faith and good works: your righteous deeds and faith in Jesus.

"Blessed are those who are invited to the marriage supper of the Lamb" (verse 9). Isn't everyone invited? Yes. "For God so loved the *world* that he gave his only Son, that *whoever* believes in him should not perish but have eternal life" (John 3:16). It is an honor and privilege and blessing just to be invited. But the greater blessing comes in the acceptance of the invitation. When the time comes, those who have persistently rejected the invitation are no longer invited. Their own rejection shuts them out.

A young father came home from work to find his little girl singing and dancing. She had been invited to her best friend's birthday party, and her mother had said she could go. Not only that, but she was going to buy her friend a present and get a new dress for herself! The next day, however, when her father came home he found her sobbing. Tragedy had struck. Her best friend had been run over by a car and killed. She had no idea of the grief this brought to her friend's family. All she knew was that her friend was gone and there would be no new dress. And no party.

When Jesus died His disciples must have been deeply grieved. Their hopes were crushed. They had been so sure that He was the Messiah and had come to establish His kingdom. Now they were equally sure it was all over. Hope was gone. There would be no party, no victory celebration. But they were wrong. It was not all over. With His resurrection came new joy. It was God's way of saying, "The party is on!" John was one of those disciples, and now he is privileged to foresee the time of celebration—the marriage supper of the Lamb and His bride. Hallelujah, indeed!

The White Horse and the King of Kings (19:11-16)

The resurrection of Jesus is also our assurance that He is coming again, just as He said He would. John now sees a vision of the conquering King's return. He is called "Faithful and True" (verse 11), "The Word of God" (verse 13), and "King of kings and Lord of lords" (verse 16). This is Jesus!

The symbols used here tell us more. The white horse reveals Him as conqueror (verse 11). His fiery eyes remind us of His perceptive judgment (verse 12). The diadems or crowns speak of His authority and royalty, while the unknown name tells us that there is still a mystery about Him and more to be learned (verse 12). The blood-soaked robe reminds us of the blood He shed for our sins (verse 13). The armies in white linen and on white horses are also conquerors, His saints who return with Him (verse 14). The sword that comes from His mouth is the Word of God, an instrument of judgment and destruction (verse 15). The iron rod and the winepress tell us of His firm rule and His furious wrath (verse 15). He is King of kings and Lord of lords, and He is coming. Look out!

The facts of the gospel are these: Jesus lived, died, arose, and is coming again. Now that is both good news and bad news. For sinners His second coming means the party is over, but for Christians it means the party is beginning. Which is it for you?

A gambler does not know if he is a winner or a loser until the match is over and the last bell has rung, the last whistle blown, or the clock has run out. Some people feel that Christianity is a gamble. Are you saved? "I sure hope so." Are you a Christian? "I try to be." Are you going to Heaven? "I won't know till I get there." We are not called to take a chance. We are called to belong to Jesus (Romans 1:6), to enjoy His peace (Colossians 3:15), to have eternal life (1 Timothy 6:12).

Jesus did not die on the cross to increase the odds that you would get to Heaven. He died on the cross to save you. "He who has the Son has life; he who has not the Son of God has not life" (1 John 5:12). It is that simple. If you are a believer in Jesus and a follower of Him you are a Christian, you are saved, you are going to Heaven.

Can you know if you are a true believer and a true follower? Yes. God has plainly revealed this in His Word. "I write this to you who believe in the name of the Son of God, that you may know that you have eternal life" (1 John 5:13). Right now by your beliefs and actions you are determining your destiny. Are you afraid to see Him coming? Or are you confidently prepared?

The Great Supper and the Lake of Fire (19:17-21)

The scene now changes from the conquering Christ and the marriage supper of the Lamb to another supper, one you don't want to attend. It is a frightening and repulsive scene that makes an Alfred Hitchcock movie like *The Birds* seem about as tame as Walt Disney's Donald Duck.

What a contrast! At the marriage supper of the Lamb the saints dine personally with Jesus. (See Revelation 3:20.) At the great supper the sinners are the feast, carrion for the vultures.

What battle is this? It is Armageddon again, from another view. It is a "no contest" kind of battle, remember? Here are the beast, the kings of the earth, and all the forces of evil assembled for battle (see Revelation 16:13-16) against the King of kings (verse 19). But the beast and the false prophet are captured and thrown into the lake of fire (verse 20), and the rest are slain and left for the birds to eat (verse 21).

All of a sudden this battle is over. There is no record of swords flashing or arrows flying or bombs bursting or of casualties incurred. The enemy is instantly and decisively defeated by the sword of the conquering King: that is, by the Word of God.

Therein lies the secret of spiritual success. The Word of God is your best defense, and offense, against sin and temptation. It provides you with armor for protection (see Ephesians 6:10-17) and the weapon for victory. Reading, studying, believing, using the Bible assures you of being a conqueror.

Christ's victory over evil will be total, final. The joy of the church, the bride, will be absolute at the marriage supper of the Lamb. The King is coming, and you are invited. If you refuse the invitation to the marriage supper of the Lamb, you *will* attend the great supper. Have you accepted His invitation? Will you now?

Blessed and holy is he who shares in the first resurrection! Over such the second death has no power, but they shall be priests of God and of Christ, and they shall reign with him a thousand years.
Revelation 20:6

Revelation 20
Reading and Study Outline

I. Four Opinions

II. The Millennial Reign (20:1-6)
Satan Is Bound (20:1-3)
The First Resurrection (20:4-6)

III. The Lost Battle (20:7-10)
Satan Is Loosed (20:7, 8)
The Lake of Fire (20:9, 10)

IV. The Great White Throne (20:11-15)
The Dead Are Judged (20:11-13)
The Second Death (20:14, 15)

The Millennium

Satan Bound 1000 Years, the Last Judgment
Revelation 20

Would you like to take part in the millennium? That is the thousand-year reign of Christ upon the earth when His saints reign with Him, during which time Satan is bound and imprisoned so that his dominion and deceptive powers are rendered ineffective.

Sound great? It is. How do I know? Because it is going on right now and I am a part of it, and you are too if you are a Christian. That's right. If you are a Christian you are part of Christ's millennial reign upon the earth right now. And when time ends and eternity begins, you will continue to reign with Him forever and ever.

Four Opinions

Perhaps we should note that not all Christians have this view. It is clear that Satan is to be restrained for a thousand years, during which Christ and His people will rule. This time is called the *millennium,* which literally means a thousand years. But the millennium has been a subject of debate for centuries. Four differing opinions have emerged, and each of them has its variations. Let's look at the four before going on with the one I prefer.

1. *The amillennial view.* The prefix *a* means *not.* In this view, the millennium is not literally just a thousand years and no more. The thousand years is a figurative term for a long time, all the time from Christ's departure to His return. This is the view that will be dis-

cussed in this chapter. Some people object to it because they find it hard to believe that Satan is chained and locked up now, when there is so much of evil in the world.

2. *The postmillennial view. Post* means *after.* This is the view of those who think Christ will come after the millennium. A hundred years ago many people thought the missionary efforts of the church were about to win the whole world, make Satan powerless, and bring in a thousand years of obedience to Christ, after which He would return in person. This view has lost much of its popularity for two reasons: First, the Scriptures seem to teach that we should be expecting Christ's return at any time, not after a thousand years of Christian world domination. Second, Christianity has not won the whole world, and anti-Christian influences seem to be gaining.

3. *The premillennial view. Pre* means *before.* Many people think the world will get worse instead of better until Jesus comes to take charge in person. They think He will come before the millennium. He will then lock up Satan and begin His reign of a thousand years. In one variation of this view it is thought that Christ will first come and take His people out of the world; then after a time of tribulation, He will return with them and begin His thousand-year reign. Some students find this view unsatisfactory because they think Christ's return will mean complete victory forever, not just for a thousand years, after which Satan will be turned loose again.

4. *The promillennial view. Pro* means *for,* in favor of. Some students are not satisfied with any of the above views. Instead of choosing one, they say, "If Satan is to be bound and Christ is to rule, we're in favor of that whenever and however it may occur!"

Now let's go on with a consideration of the amillennial view, the first of the four listed above.

The Millennial Reign (20:1-6)

Satan is bound in chains for one thousand years (verses 1-3). The use of symbolic language here is immediately obvious. How can a powerful spiritual being like Satan be locked in literal links of steel? Something far more powerful is required. Satan has been chained and bound by the person and power of Jesus Christ, particularly by His death on the cross. This has rendered Satan powerless and ineffective against those in whom Christ lives.

Jesus spoke of this phenomenon during His ministry. "Or how can one enter a strong man's house and plunder his goods, unless he first binds the strong man? Then indeed he may plunder his house"

The Amillennial View

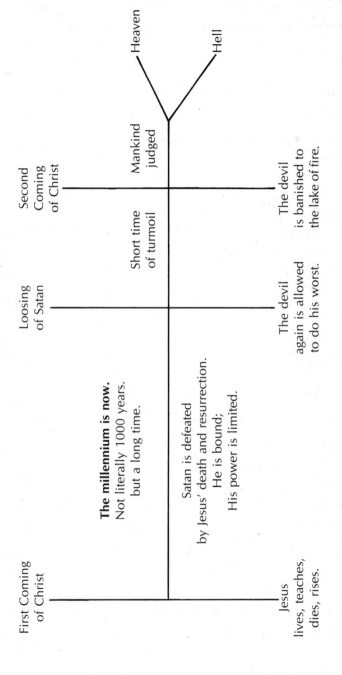

The Postmillennial View

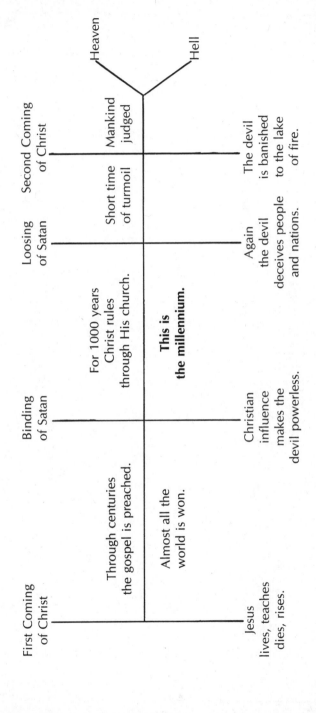

The Premillennial View

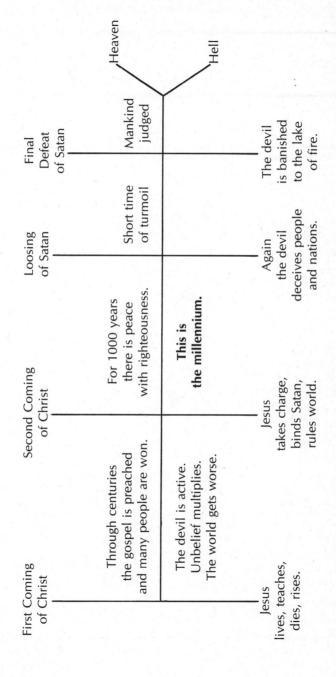

First Coming of Christ

Jesus lives, teaches, dies, rises.

Through centuries the gospel is preached and many people are won.

The devil is active. Unbelief multiplies. The world gets worse.

Second Coming of Christ

Jesus takes charge, binds Satan, rules world.

For 1000 years there is peace with righteousness.

This is the millennium.

Loosing of Satan

Again the devil deceives people and nations.

Short time of turmoil

Final Defeat of Satan

The devil is banished to the lake of fire.

Mankind judged

Heaven

Hell

(Matthew 12:29). It was by the binding of Satan that Jesus was able to perform His ministry. He plundered Satan's house by driving out the demons who served Satan (Matthew 12:22-29) and by releasing Satan's prisoners (Luke 13:10-16). And it is by the binding of Satan that we are able to be saved and to live the Christian life. Jesus also prophesied that at the time of His death "shall the ruler of this world be cast out" (John 12:28-33).

How long will this "thousand years" actually be? It represents a period of time known only to God. "But do not ignore this one fact, beloved, that with the Lord one day is as a thousand years, and a thousand years as one day" (2 Peter 3:8). One thousand symbolizes completeness. It does not always mean an exact number. "For every beast of the forest is mine, the cattle on a thousand hills" (Psalm 50:10). If "a thousand" must mean exactly one thousand, then what about all the cattle on all the other hills? Whose are they? They too are God's, of course. "A thousand hills" means all the hills, and "a thousand years" can mean all the years from the life of Christ on earth until He comes again. Satan is prevented from defeating and destroying you throughout all the time that you are a faithful follower of Jesus Christ.

Christians are still tempted after they accept Christ. How can Satan be so active and powerful if he is bound? Russell Boatman illustrates this well in *What the Bible Says About the End Time*. He recalls that Jimmy Hoffa in a federal prison continued to exercise great influence in and through a labor union. Likewise Satan imprisoned in "the pit" can and does continue to operate. He sends out delegates or emissaries, utilizes bribes and threats, and tries to tempt others into the cage with him. But don't be deceived. He can't destroy you unless you cooperate with him. If you resist him he will flee from you (James 4:7). He is not allowed to use any temptation that you cannot overcome if you do your best (1 Corinthians 10:13). Put on the whole armor of God, and Satan's fiery darts are rendered ineffective against you (Ephesians 6:16). Nothing, not even powers and principalities, can separate you from the love of God in Jesus Christ (Romans 8:38, 39). Thank God, Satan is bound!

So now it is possible for us who are in Christ, who have experienced the first resurrection, to reign with Him throughout the millennium (verses 4-6). To whom is judgment committed? (verse 4). To all saints, according to 1 Corinthians 6:2. And what John now envisions is a panorama of all believers: those who have been faithful unto death, even though beheaded; those who have refused to wor-

Bound but Busy
Revelation 20:1-3

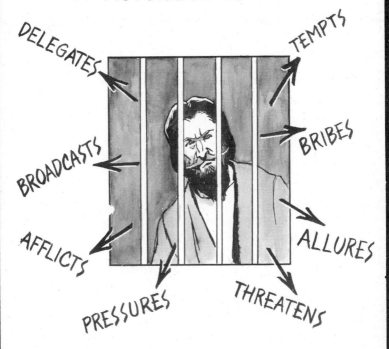

DELEGATES

TEMPTS

BROADCASTS

BRIBES

AFFLICTS

ALLURES

PRESSURES

THREATENS

Critics of the amillennial theory find it hard to believe that Satan is chained and locked in the pit at the same time he is going about like a roaring lion (1 Peter 5:8). Advocates of the theory respond that one in prison can still be powerful. For example, John the Baptist in prison continued to have an influence as his disciples were free and in contact with many people (Luke 5:33). John's influence was good, but in like manner the devil can exert an evil influence even if he is in prison. His disciples are at large (Matthew 13:38). Certainly Satan's influence is strong in many ways, as the sketch suggests. But still he is bound in the sense that his influence and power are limited. He is not allowed to bring you any temptation you cannot resist if you do your best (1 Corinthians 10:13).

ship the beast or its image; those who have not received its mark (verse 4). All Christians are to participate in judgment. All Christians are to be faithful unto death and refuse the mark. All Christians have experienced the first resurrection. And all Christians reign with Christ, now and forever.

"The first resurrection" refers to the death to sin and the resurrection to new life in Christ. Paul refers to this death and resurrection in his treatise on baptism. (Read Romans 6:1-11.) Baptism depicts the burial of the dead person as he is lowered into the water and his resurrection as he is raised out of the water. Baptism is an active and visible participation in the new birth as an expression of faith and as an act of obedience. "We were buried therefore with him by baptism into death, so that as Christ was raised from the dead by the glory of the Father, we too might walk in newness of life" (Romans 6:4).

All Christians are priests (verse 6; compare 1 Peter 2:5, 9). All Christians share in the first resurrection. All Christians have been made free from the second death. And all Christians reign with Christ for one thousand years, throughout the millennium (verse 6). Satan is bound now. The reign of the church over sin and death is now. The millennium is now.

The Last Battle (20:7-10)

The millennium is ended. Satan is now loosed to deceive the nations and to gather his armies for battle. He is finally given unlimited freedom, but it will last only a "little while" (verse 3). The end result will be the destruction of his power. The last battle between righteousness and evil will soon be fought, and the outcome is predetermined. This is yet one more prediction of the battle of Armageddon, and one more time God assures us that it will be "no contest." Satan and his followers will be easily and quickly defeated.

They come from the four corners of the earth, from Gog and Magog (verse 8). They surround the holy city ready to do battle, but the battle never takes place. Instead, they are consumed by fire from heaven (verse 9). This is when the devil is totally defeated, his work is halted, his influence is ended, and he is cast into the lake of fire (verse 10).

The torment of Hell for Satan and his followers is eternal. How can this be? How can a good and loving God be so unforgiving and merciless? The question reminds me of a concept of God expressed by Omar Khayyam:

The Millennium

Revelation 20

Verses	Feature	Meaning	Scriptures
2-7	1000 years	The Christian era	2 Peter 3:8 Psalm 50:10; 90:4
2	Satan bound	Rendered powerless by Jesus' life and death	Matthew 12:22-29 John 12:29-33
3	No more deception	Christians are warned, empowered, protected.	Ephesians 6:10-18 James 4:7
4	Judgment and rule	All Christians share	1 Corinthians 6:2 Revelation 5:10
4-6	First resurrection	From dead in sin to new life—conversion; baptism	Romans 6:1-11 Ephesians 2:1-7
7	Satan loosed	Free to deceive nations but only for a short time	Revelation 20:7-10

> There are those who tell
> Of a God who flings to hell
> The reckless pots he marred in making.
> Pshaw! He's a good fellow,
> And twill all be well.

God is more than "a good fellow." He is a just and wise God who has revealed the truth about eternity to us. There is a Heaven and there is a Hell, and you are free to choose your eternal destiny. He has warned us against Hell, and He has done everything possible to save us for Heaven, even to the extreme of allowing His only Son to die on the cross as a sacrifice for our sins. What love! What mercy! God does not choose for some to be saved and for others to go to Hell. His desire, according to His Word, is that none should perish but that all should repent (2 Peter 3:9). But the choice is yours.

The Great White Throne (20:11-15)

The dead are now judged before the great white throne of God (verses 11-13). The implication of verse 11 is that there is no place to hide. Finally it is just man and God, face to face.

Everyone who ever lived must stand before the great white throne. "For we must all appear before the judgment seat of Christ, so that each one may receive good or evil, according to what he has done in the body" (2 Corinthians 5:10). But for the believer this holds no terror; there is no judgment enacted against him. "He who hears my word and believes him who sent me," Jesus said, "has eternal life; he does not come into judgment, but has passed from death to life" (John 5:24). In other words, there is no judgment of condemnation for those who are in Christ (Romans 8:1).

What are the criteria for judgment? All were judged by what they had done (verse 12). We are judged by our works or deeds, by what we do or do not do here on earth. The righteous are clothed in their good deeds (Revelation 19:8), while the wicked are condemned for their sinful deeds. Are we not saved by faith? Of course we are, but faith and works are inseparable. Faith must find expression in works or it is not really faith at all (James 2:14-17). We are saved by faith, but we are judged by works. We are held accountable both for what we believe and what we do.

The wicked include every one whose "name was not found written in the book of life" (verse 15). They are thrown into the lake of fire along with Death and Hades. This is where the devil, the beast, and the false prophet are also cast (verse 10; 19:20). Hades, the abode of the dead, now meets its eternal fate. It can have no further use, for even Death receives this final destruction. It is according to Paul's prophecy: "The last enemy to be destroyed is death" (1 Corinthians 15:26).

Eternal, never-ending suffering and prolonged spiritual death may be unthinkable, but they are true. Many times Jesus refers to the exclusion, the darkness, the pain, and the fire of Hell. In the parable of the sheep and goats, for example, the King says to those on His left, "Depart from me, you cursed, into the eternal fire prepared for the devil and his angels" (Matthew 25:41). "And they will go away into eternal punishment, but the righteous into eternal life" (Matthew 25:46). God is being entirely open and honest with us. We have been fairly forewarned.

The question remains, how do I get my name written in the book of life? That is really what this book is all about. That is the "bottom line," so to speak. First I must renounce this world with all of its wickedness. I must turn from sin by repenting, and I must turn to God. I must identify completely with the person of Jesus Christ through faith in Him, in baptism, and by continuing good works. When you accept Jesus as your Lord and Savior your name is written there, and you are His forever!

Then I saw a new heaven and a new earth; for the first heaven and the first earth had passed away, and the sea was no more.

And I saw the holy city, new Jerusalem, coming down out of heaven from God, prepared as a bride adorned for her husband.

Revelation 21:1, 2

Revelation 21:1—22:5
Reading and Study Outline

The Beginning of Forever

A New Heaven and a New Earth
Revelation 21:1–22:5

"Today is the first day of the rest of your life." That is an appealing and sentimental notion, and it has sold a lot of posters and a lot of coffee mugs! There will come a day, however, that will be the first day of the rest of your life in a more dramatic way. It will be the first day of eternity, the beginning of forever. And what a day it will be!

True, your life is already eternal if you are a Christian. In a sense, eternity has already begun. But you know the earthly phase of your life will end and the Heavenly phase will begin. This mortal will put on immortality (1 Corinthians 15:53) and start a new life in a new environment. That is what we are calling the first day of eternity.

How much do you know about Heaven? Try the following True-False quiz just for fun. Study each question carefully before answering. Notice exactly what is said, and then put a check mark under *T* for true or *F* for false.

T	*F*	
____	____	1. The street of Heaven is paved with gold.
____	____	2. Each gate to Heaven is made of pearls.
____	____	3. Heaven's gates are open only in the day, but they are never closed.
____	____	4. In the center of the city is a temple.
____	____	5. Heavenly gold is transparent.

The answers to these questions are in the above text and will be pointed out in this chapter. If you watch for them you can see whether your answers are correct or not.

Of course it is possible to argue that the new Jerusalem is not Heaven at all, but a feature of the new earth announced in Revelation 21:1. John in his vision did see it coming down out of heaven. For this study let's just bypass the question of location. In the new Jerusalem God's people will live with Him in perfect happiness (21:3, 4). Traditionally it has been called Heaven, and we have used that name in the quiz above. You may call it new Jerusalem if you prefer.

The New Heaven and New Earth (21:1-8)

The millennial reign of the church with Christ has now come to an end. The devil, Death, and Hades have been cast into the lake of fire, along with all those whose names are not written in the book of life. God's judgment is complete. This is the beginning of forever, the start of that phase of existence that will not end.

At this point in time (which may be called beyond time), the earth, heaven, and sea as we now know them have totally disappeared. They have ceased to exist (verse 1). Now there are no more tears or pain or death (verse 4). The old order has ended, the new has begun. The new order is characterized by a new heaven, a new earth, the holy city, and a new intimacy between God and man (verses 1-3). God's original intention in creation is finally realized. There is perfect fellowship between creature and Creator.

Everything is new: the people, the place, the relationships (verses 5-8). Every Christian has been preparing for this since first accepting Jesus as Lord. "Therefore, if any one is in Christ, he is a new creation; the old has passed away, behold, the new has come" (2 Corinthians 5:17). The new life in Christ now reaches perfection. "It is done!" God declares (verse 6). This is final. The conquerors are rewarded with the fountain of life (verse 6), while the wicked receive what their earthly life-style has demanded—the second death (verse 8).

The list of those who are cast into the lake of fire deserves scrutiny. For the most part it is expected: "the polluted, . . . murderers, fornicators, sorcerers, idolaters, and all liars" (verse 8). But also listed are "the faithless." Conceivably these could be morally good people, but without faith in Jesus they are hopelessly lost. The "cowardly" are on the list, too. Is cowardice a sin? Yes, if it is the cowardice that fears to take a stand for Jesus and remain faithful to Him no matter what life may bring. Christianity requires both faith and courage.

When Jesus comes again and eternity begins, it will mean either reward or punishment for every person who ever lived. You, personally, will one day drink of the fountain of life or burn in the lake of fire. God has repeated that point too many times for us to miss it.

What does all this mean in terms of how we should live now? How we should conduct ourselves this week? Today? The question is asked and answered in 2 Peter 3:10-13.

> But the day of the Lord will come like a thief, and then the heavens will pass away with a loud noise, and the elements will be dissolved with fire, and the earth and the works that are upon it will be burned up.
>
> Since all these things are thus to be dissolved, what sort of persons ought you to be in lives of holiness and godliness, waiting for and hastening the coming of the day of God, because of which the heavens will be kindled and dissolved, and the elements will melt with fire! But according to his promise we wait for new heavens and a new earth in which righteousness dwells.

The coming end of the world means that we should be living holy and godly lives, committed to righteous living. "Waiting for and hastening the coming of the day of God" means being ready and helping others to get ready for Christ's coming. You get yourself ready by committing your life to Jesus and living according to His will. You help others get ready by leading them to Christ, bringing them to church, introducing them to the Christian life. Please hurry up and get ready. The task is urgent and the time is short.

The Holy City (21:9-21)

There are five things to be noted in this passage about our everlasting home. First is the identity of the holy city. It is the new Jerusalem, which is also the bride of Christ (verses 9-11 and verse 2). We know from Ephesians 5:21-33 that the bride of Christ is the church. It seems that this spotless city is a symbol of God's church perfected.

Second is the symbolism of the great wall, standing 216 feet tall (verses 12, 17). That is higher than a twenty-story building! The Great Wall of China at its highest point is less than fifty feet high. Why must new Jerusalem have a wall so incredibly high? In old

Jerusalem the wall represented safety and security. This Heavenly wall represents absolute, unconditional safety and security—eternal security, if you will.

Third are the twelve gates and the twelve foundations. The gates bear the names of the twelve tribes of Israel, and the twelve foundations bear the names of the twelve apostles (verses 12-15). This is reminiscent of the twenty-four elders (4:4). The holy city involves both the Old and the New Covenants. All of God's people are welcome here, both Jews and Gentiles.

Fourth is the size of the city. It is twelve thousand stadia, or fifteen hundred miles, long and wide and high. Does that sound small? Try a little comparison. The city in the United States with the largest land area is Oklahoma City, which is approximately twenty-five miles long and about twenty-five miles wide. Now imagine that somehow it could be built to extend twenty-five miles high. That's big! But the Heavenly city is fifteen hundred miles in each direction, sixty times as long and wide and high. Such a city would spread from Chicago to the middle of Mexico, and tower into outer space. However, I take the measurements to be spiritually symbolic rather than describing an earthly, physical size. John saw an immense city, with space more than adequate for the people of God.

Fifth, we must take note of all those jewels, the pearls, and the gold. Solomon in all of his glory never knew, nor could he even have imagined, such splendor. This is the attempt to convey through the limitations of human experience and language the incredible, unspeakable, magnificent wealth and beauty of Heaven. It is alluring above all the actual wealth that earth can offer. "What will it profit a man, if he gains the whole world and forfeits his life [his soul]?" (Matthew 16:26). I can hardly wait!

The city is made of pure gold, clear as glass (verse 18), and so is the street (verse 21). (The answer to quiz question number 1 is True. The answer to number 5 also is True.) The foundations of the wall around the city are "adorned with every jewel" (verse 19). There are twelve gates, and each gate is made of a single pearl (verse 21). (The answer to number 2 is False. Each gate is made of a pearl, not pearls.)

Who ever heard of transparent gold? The only thing I can think of in our earthly experience that might compare is golden light like, perhaps, a laser beam. But again I believe that Heaven will be more beautiful, exciting, and intriguing than anything we now know or even imagine.

The holy city would stretch from Chicago to the middle of Mexico, and tower into outer space.

Tourists pay out millions of dollars annually to tour mansions and castles and to admire collections of antiques, art, and jewels. Heaven is all this and more, too! Jesus has gone there to prepare a place just for you. In fact, it will all be yours to enjoy, including fellowship with the Father. And the admission price? It is a free gift from God through His Son Jesus.

The Glory of God (21:22-27)

At the heart of Jewish life and faith was the temple in Jerusalem. But in the new Jerusalem there is no temple (verse 22). (The answer to quiz question number four is False.) Why not? The temple was the place to draw near to God and to worship Him. In Heaven, however, God is the temple. Heaven is a place of constant intimacy with Him (verse 3) and of continuous worship.

Heaven's gates are open all day, but since there is no night there (verse 25), they are never closed! (The answer to quiz question number 3 is True.) There is neither sun nor moon, only the glory of God along with whatever inferior glory man may have contributed (verses 23, 24). Heaven is always bright and beautiful—no gloomy days or depressing weather. The absence of night may also suggest that there is no need for sleep—no weariness or fatigue. Neither is there anything there that is unclean (verse 27)—no evil and no temptations. What a glorious place indeed!

Does it seem a bit strange to you that a city should have such a great, high wall (symbolizing security) and then leave its gates open all the time? Heaven is no literal fortress, of course, as if it might sometime be assailed by armies. The enemy has been destroyed; there is no danger of attack. The wall is only a symbol. The real security Christians have is in their personal relationship with God through Jesus.

The open gates therefore do not represent a threat to security. There are twelve of them, never closed, three facing in each direction. They symbolize the openness of God, His accessibility to man. Heaven itself is attainable. The open gates stand as an open invitation to all who will believe in Jesus Christ and follow Him.

The Return to Paradise (22:1-5)

The river is the symbol of life (verse 1). The tree also symbolizes life, with its fruit for food (twelve varieties) and its leaves for healing (verse 2). Does this mean that there are thirst and hunger and sickness in Heaven? Quite to the contrary! The river and the tree indicate the permanent absence of any such deficiencies. Heaven is totally satisfying and fulfilling.

Gathered around the throne of God and of the Lamb are His servants (verse 3). These are they who have His name written on their foreheads (verse 4), not just the 144,000 (Revelation 7:3-8), but all who have been marked and sealed with the Holy Spirit. (See notes on "The 144,000 and the Innumerable Multitude" in chapter 4 of this book.) His servants are there worshiping Him (verse 3) and reigning with Him (verse 5). There we shall see Him face to face! (verse 4).

Here, then, is man's return to Paradise. John's vision reminds us of that first paradise, the Garden of Eden. There was the tree of life (Genesis 2:9) and the river (Genesis 2:10) and the presence of God himself, "walking in the garden in the cool of the day" (Genesis 3:8). Paradise was lost when man sinned, but it was regained when Christ died on the cross. Now man can find his ultimate destiny and fulfillment and become all God meant and created him to be. When we accept Jesus our sins are forgiven. We are restored to the image of God and are given the right to dwell with Him in Heaven forever. We can eat of the tree and drink of the river and walk with Him in the cool of the day.

Behold, I am coming soon, bringing my recompense, to repay every one for what he has done.

Revelation 22:12

Revelation 22:6-21
Reading and Study Outline

I. The Call to Obedience (22:6-9)
"Keep the words of this book."

II. The Call to Holiness (22:10-15)
"Wash your robes and live."

III. The Call to Faith (22:16-20)
"I am coming soon."

IV. The End (22:21)
"Amen."

Last Call

Christ's Imminent Return and Final Invitation
Revelation 22:6-21

This message was painted on the side of an evangelist's van: "Where will you spend eternity? Most people don't decide until the eleventh hour. Our service begins at 10:30."

We are living in the last days (Acts 2:17). In fact, "it is the last hour" (1 John 2:18). In this text (Revelation 22:6-21) Jesus says three times, "I am coming soon." Time is running out! This is the final invitation, the last call.

The Call to Obedience (22:6-9)

The last call is a call to obedience: "Blessed is he who keeps the words of the prophecy of this book" (verse 7). The events here revealed to John "must soon take place" (verse 6). They were not destined for some distant time, but would begin even in his own lifetime: for example, the tribulation he shared (Revelation 1:9).

Three times Jesus said, "I am coming soon." The first time is recorded in verse 7. It increases the urgency of the call to obedience, to keep the words of this book. The purpose of the book of Revelation was stated very clearly in the beginning and has been consistent throughout: "Blessed is he who reads aloud the words of the prophecy, and blessed are those who hear, and who *keep what is written therein;* for the time is near" (Revelation 1:3). God wants obedience!

An essential part of that obedience is worship. Twice John tries to worship an angel (verses 8, 9; 19:10). But the angel's directive is very clear: "Worship God." At the heart of our obedience to God is our faithfulness in worship.

Jesus is coming soon. How do you know if you are ready for His coming? You will be ready if you accept His call to obedience. Commit yourself to church membership and gather regularly for worship. Read, study, and keep His Word. Don't be guilty of listening to the sermon and then immediately forgetting what it was all about. Plan to put it into practice.

Dennis the Menace is shown walking with his parents to church one Sunday morning. On the way he calls out to his friend, "We're on the way to church now, Joey, but I'll be myself again after lunch." The "self" God calls you to be is an obedient, serving, worshiping Christian, both in and out of church—before, during, and after. As James so aptly put it, "But be doers of the word, and not hearers only, deceiving yourselves" (James 1:22).

The Call to Holiness (22:10-15)

Second, the last call is a call to holiness: "Blessed are those who wash their robes" (verse 14). This call to holy living is an invitation that is open to all. Revelation is not a closed book; it is not to be sealed up (verse 10). It was John's responsibility to record what was revealed to him and deliver it to the churches. It is your responsibility to keep the message open and available. Whatever you have learned or received from God in this study of Revelation, pass on to others, by all means! Don't seal it up in your mind and heart.

"Let the evildoer still do evil" (verse 11) may sound like approval of continued sinning. Of course it is not. God allows for evil, but He does not approve it. He gives us the freedom to do good or to do evil, but warns us of the eternal consequences. If you choose to disobey God and to do evil and be filthy, then that will be your condition for all eternity, separated from the holy God whom you have rejected. But if you repent and are cleansed of your unrighteousness, and choose to live a life of holiness, purity, and righteousness, then that will be your condition for all eternity, in fellowship with God. The choice is yours.

Again Jesus states, "I am coming soon" (verse 12) and identifies himself as the eternal God, the Alpha and the Omega (verse 13; Revelation 1:8). Those who have washed their robes (verse 14) "and made them white in the blood of the Lamb" (Revelation 7:14), are inside the gates and have access to the tree of life. They are the pure and the holy. But the unclean, the unholy, are on the outside where there are darkness, weeping, and gnashing of teeth (Matthew 22:13). And there they will ever remain.

Jesus is coming soon. How do you know if you are ready for His coming? You will be ready if you accept His call to holiness. If you are morally clean, forgiven, washed in the blood of the Lamb, then and only then are you ready. "Come now, let us reason together, says the Lord: though your sins are like scarlet, they shall be as white as snow; though they are red like crimson, they shall become like wool" (Isaiah 1:18). That may defy human logic, but it is the way God has reasoned it out. Believe it. Live the Christian life, the life of holiness, and you are ready for Christ's coming.

The Call to Faith (22:16-20)

The last call, finally, is a call to faith, a call to put absolute trust in the Lord who for the third time announces, "Surely I am coming soon" (verse 20). There are two calls in this text. The first is God's call to us. By His Spirit, the Spirit of Jesus, and through His bride, the church, the invitation is extended, "Come" (verse 17). All of us who hear and obey that invitation are then to extend it on to others, ad infinitum till Jesus comes.

The terms of the invitation are quite simple as given here. If you are thirsty—really desire Christ and His forgiveness and eternity— then these are yours free for the asking (verse 17). The offer does carry a warning label, however. God's terms of salvation, indeed all of His revelation, as stated throughout His book, must be taken as is (verses 18, 19). Don't try to change God's conditions, even in the least detail.

The second aspect of this call to faith is represented by our call to God. I am thinking of John's response to the Lord when he says, "Amen. Come, Lord Jesus!" (verse 20). What a magnificent prayer! What faith! He is boldly affirming Jesus' plan to return again soon, and he is in complete agreement with it. There is no fear or intimidation, only confidence and anticipation. It is as if John were saying, "Come on, Lord. I'm ready when You are." That is the faith that every Christian may voice with equal enthusiasm and confidence.

Jesus is coming soon. How do you know if you are ready for His coming? You will be ready if you accept His call to faith. "Believe in the Lord Jesus, and you will be saved" (Acts 16:31). This is no empty faith of words (see Matthew 7:21). Rather it is a faith of both believing and obeying by living the life of holiness to which Christ has called us. Armed with that kind of faith we are ready to join with John in the happy refrain, "Amen. Come, Lord Jesus."

The End (22:21)

The beautiful prayer completes the record of Jesus' revelation to John. God's grace is sufficient for our every need. His grace is most certainly with His saints. It is by His unmerited favor and help and blessings that we are saved, that we live the Christian life, and that we go to Heaven. It is this grace that He invites you to accept. It is His last call.

> Church is finally over,
>   I'm headed for the door.
> The sermon was inspiring
>   like hundreds were before.
> The choir sang the anthem
>   the best I've ever heard,
> And all the people list'ning
>   were blest and even stirred.
> The invitation given
>   was earnest, warm, and strong
>   while all the congregation
>   joined in the final song.
> I almost was persuaded
>   to let the Savior in
>   but church is finally over
>   I turned away again.
>
> Church is finally over
>   I feel almost the same.
> I guess I'll wait 'til next time
>   to call upon His name.
> They say He's very patient,
>   long-suffering and kind.
> His arms are always open
>   and those who seek shall find.
> I've heard the gospel story
>   until I know it well
>   how Jesus died to save me
>   from everlasting hell.

Yet I can't help but wonder
when my last chance will be
and church is finally over
for all eternity.*

What follows Revelation 22:21? In my Bible there is only a blank page, nothing more. This is the final invitation, the last call. We are living in the last days, and Jesus is coming soon. Great suffering and punishment and eternal Hell lie ahead for the wicked and the unbelieving. Great grace and glory and the presence of God lie ahead for the saints. Are you ready?

Soon
it
will
be
THE END